HOW TO FIND THE RIGHT COLLEGE
A WORKBOOK FOR PARENTS OF HIGH SCHOOL STUDENTS

Regina H. Paul and Marie G. Segares
Co-Hosts of *NYCollegeChat*

A publication of
Policy Studies in Education
*A nonprofit organization with over 40 years of success
in engaging parents and school boards in education*

How To Find the Right College: A Workbook for Parents of High School Students
by Regina H. Paul and Marie G. Segares

Published by Policy Studies in Education, Great Neck, New York

Ordering Information:
Books may be purchased in quantity by contacting the publisher, Policy Studies in Education, by mail (25 Great Neck Road, Great Neck, New York 11021) or by email (info@policystudies.org).

Library of Congress Control Number: 2015944469
ISBN 978-0-9864088-0-9 (ebook)
ISBN 978-0-9864088-1-6 (print book)
10 9 8 7 6 5 4 3 2 1
1. Education/Parent Participation
2. Education/Counseling/General
3. Family & Relationships/Life Stages/Teenagers

First Edition
Printed in the United States of America

Contents

So, How Can This Workbook Help You?

The world of college is incredibly complex—and that assessment comes from two people who have spent a total of 50 years working with and for colleges. We can't imagine what it must seem like to parents of high school students.

Collectively, we have done consulting projects for well over a hundred colleges and have taught for colleges both on campus and online in the U.S. and abroad. We have also worked with hundreds of high schools across the U.S. to prepare students for college and careers.

Together with Principal Chris Aguirre in 2009, we co-founded an innovative Early College high school in Brooklyn, where regular New York City public school students finished their high school graduation requirements in just three years instead of the traditional four. We had the privilege of advising several hundred of our students and their parents as those teenagers took their first steps into college—most of them, a year early.

It was a humbling experience. We realized that there were some things we absolutely didn't know. It also turned out that we were wrong about some things we thought we knew very well. If we couldn't keep up with the changing world of college when we were out there in it, how could a guidance counselor in a high school or a parent at home?

Our current projects come out of our experience at that New York City high school and the kinds of conversations we had with our parents and students. We started with a podcast, *NYCollegeChat*, because we thought a podcast might be easily accessible to busy parents, who could listen in their cars or on the train or in the subway—or just at home while they were getting other stuff done. After about six months of weekly podcast episodes, we realized that virtually everything we said was just as useful to parents outside New York City and New York State as it was to our original audience (we recently welcomed our first listeners in Europe).

Finally, it occurred to us to put our advice into print to reach parents who would rather read than listen. And so this workbook for parents was born.

We believe that understanding all of the options in the world of college (including all of the ones you have never considered) is the first step toward helping your teenager find the right college. Understanding what your "deal breakers" are is the second step.

By the way, we are confident that there is a college out there (and, undoubtedly, more than one) that is a good fit for your teenager, even if you all haven't heard of it yet. We hope that this workbook can help you find the one you're looking for.

Regina H. Paul
Marie G. Segares

July, 2015

[1]

Public, Private, and Proprietary Colleges

THIS CHAPTER LOOKS AT how colleges are funded and what that means for the tuition you will have to pay for your teenager. We hate to start by talking about money, but it is likely that financial considerations are the basis of college-going decisions for many, many students in the U.S. today. We wish that were not the case. We wish that your discussion at home could simply be about which college is best for your teenager, based on the merits of the college and the merits of your teenager. But a look at public *vs.* private *vs.* proprietary colleges might, in fact, be the very first decision you have to make.

Public Colleges

Public colleges are paid for, at least in part, by state and local governments—that means, by taxes—primarily for the benefit of their own residents. As a result, public colleges have reasonably low—and sometimes very low—tuition for state and local residents, but nonresidents have to pay more. That makes sense because their taxes didn't pay for them.

States fund public colleges, and all states have public colleges. New York, for example, has one huge public college system: The State University of New York, commonly referred to as SUNY (pronounced SUE-knee), with its 64 two-year and four-year campuses spread across the state. Some states have more than one system of public colleges, like California with its University of California campuses (California's premier public system), its California State University campuses (the second tier of public colleges in California), and its California Community Colleges System campuses (the third tier of public colleges in California, offering opportunities to an enormous number of California students who do not have the high school grades and/or the financial resources and/or the inclination to attend one of California's public four-year campuses).

Some local governments, like big cities and counties, can afford to help fund their own public higher education, with the rest of the funding typically provided by the state government. For example, the Dallas County Community College District has seven community college campuses in and around Dallas, and The City University of New York, commonly referred to as CUNY (pronounced CUE-knee), has 24 campuses spread across the five boroughs of New York City. Furthermore, because New York State funds contribute to the operation of CUNY campuses, any New York State resident can attend a CUNY campus in New York City at the resident tuition rate, after completing the appropriate paperwork.

Interestingly, even though public colleges are supported with a lot of tax dollars, student tuition is still a major source of revenue. That's why they are not totally free to attend. Even public colleges need student tuition dollars to stay open. There has been a lot about that in the news lately as one state after another has talked about raising the tuition at its public colleges, and there will probably continue to be more such talk in the years ahead.

Because public colleges have lower tuition rates than private colleges, the cost of sending your teenager to a public college is likely lower than sending him or her to a private college. Of course, if a student is awarded a generous scholarship by a private college, that could bring tuition down—maybe to a public college level, maybe even lower. But, students can be awarded scholarships by public colleges, too, making the cost of attending a public college even more attractive. While scholarships can certainly help you finance your teenager's college education, you can't count on them. They are hard to get, even for the best students. So if money is the main issue for you, finding your teenager a number of good public college options is probably your first step.

What if you are an out-of-state student and want to study at a great public university in another state? You can do it, but you are likely to have to meet higher admissions standards than in-state residents, and you will most likely have to pay more for the privilege. Some states with popular public colleges limit the number of out-of-state students they will take in order to leave ample room for their own residents—even though out-of-staters bring in more dollars. As budget woes grow in various states, you can continue to read in the news about how states are dealing with this conflict.

So, what are some great public colleges? There are a lot of websites and national ranking systems of colleges that are available to help you answer that question. However, anyone's list of truly great public colleges would include a relatively small college whose name sounds as though it were private: the College of William & Mary in Virginia, the second-oldest college in the U.S. That list would also include quite large (sometimes really huge) state universities of the kind that populate the North, South, Midwest, and West, but not so much the Northeast: the University of Michigan, University of Wisconsin–Madison, University of Minnesota, University of Iowa, University of Virginia, University of North Carolina at Chapel Hill, University of Texas at Austin, University of Washington, and University of California, Berkeley, to name a few that no one would argue about. That list would include one well-known state university with a technical twist: Georgia Institute of Technology (commonly referred to as Georgia Tech). To be sure, that list would also include the five U.S. military service academies, funded by the federal government rather than by the states in which they are located.

Creating lists of great colleges is a difficult and thankless task, and there are certainly many others that should be listed in this paragraph. This was just to get you started. Check out a variety of websites for such lists and know that there are wonderful public colleges out there for your teenager. (In fact, you might want to listen to our podcast's Series 4: Looking at Colleges Outside Your Comfort Zone, which is a virtual tour of a couple hundred public and private colleges spread across the U.S. and which spotlights great public colleges in every region of the country.)

If you live in New York State, where we started our podcast, you know that New York State does not have quite the same tradition of big state universities as states in other regions of the country. New York is not a state where huge numbers of high school seniors are excited about heading to the flagship state university campus, where they can study just about anything at the undergraduate or graduate level, can play on competitive sports teams of all kinds, can join clubs of all sorts, and can have an active social life besides— like The Ohio State University in Columbus or Pennsylvania State University in State College or the University of Colorado Boulder or the University of Mississippi (commonly referred to as Ole Miss) in Oxford. While New York doesn't have one super-popular flag-ship state university campus like that, we would argue that Stony Brook University (the State University of New York at Stony Brook, located on Long Island) is perhaps New York's premier public uni-versity—an institution that can hold its own academically with any public university anywhere.

As we leave our discussion of public colleges, just remember that going to a public college in another state will cost you more than going to a public college in your own state, but still might cost you less than going to a private college anywhere else.

Private Colleges

Since we are proud alumnae of private colleges, it seems only right that we should say something positive about them. Private colleges, which are funded by the tuition of their students and by donations from their alumni/alumnae and others, are often seen as being more prestigious or as being "better" colleges than public colleges. The fact is that many private colleges are indeed better than some public colleges; another fact is that many public colleges are indeed better than some private colleges.

What could "better" mean? Students are smarter? Professors are better educated? Classes are smaller? Extracurricular activities are more available? Campuses are more beautiful? Campus facil-ities are more impressive? Alumni/alumnae are more successful?

7

The fact is that some public colleges beat some private colleges on all these measures, so it pays to know as much as you can about what various public and private colleges have to offer your teenager.

Just as with great public colleges, there are a lot of websites and national ranking systems available to help you identify great private colleges. When looking at college rankings, remember that different ranking systems base their rankings on different factors—some of which might be of no interest to you or your teenager. So look at them if you wish, but keep in mind that rankings won't tell you how your teenager will fit into that campus—academically or socially—and it's that "fit" that will determine just how happy he or she will be.

So what are some great private colleges? That list would certainly include a host of traditional and relatively small liberal arts colleges: Kenyon College, Oberlin College, Hamilton College, Skidmore College, Haverford College, Swarthmore College, Pomona College, Carleton College, Middlebury College, Bowdoin College, Vassar College, Smith College, Wellesley College, Amherst College, and Williams College, to name just a few. That list would also include the well-known eight Ivy League schools: the University of Pennsylvania, Columbia University, Cornell University, Princeton University, Brown University, Harvard University, Yale University, and Dartmouth College. It would also include Barnard College, which is in its own category because it is a private women's college affiliated with Columbia University. And let's not forget other large private universities: the Massachusetts Institute of Technology, Stanford University, New York University, University of Chicago, Johns Hopkins University, Duke University, Boston University, Georgetown University, Emory University, Northwestern

University, Rice University, and University of Southern California, to name but some. Many alumni/alumnae of private colleges and universities like these believe that they got what they paid for, and many undoubtedly did (and many also had financial aid and scholarships to help cover the costs).

One thing to keep in mind: Names can be deceiving. Some public colleges sound as though they are private and *vice versa*. For example, colleges that use the names of states: New York University and the University of Pennsylvania sound public (like the University of Arizona or the University of Illinois), but they are private. Or colleges that use the names of cities: The University of Pittsburgh is public, but the University of Rochester is private. So be sure to double check as you and your teenager look at colleges.

Public–Private Partnerships

Earlier, we listed Cornell University among its Ivy League counterparts as being private. However, Cornell is a special case and one that should be especially attractive to New York residents. With its main campus upstate in Ithaca, Cornell offers seven schools/ colleges to choose from at the undergraduate level—four that are private and three that are actually public. The four private ones are the College of Architecture, Art, and Planning; the College of Arts and Sciences; the College of Engineering; and the School of Hotel Administration. The three public ones were established by an Act of the New York State Legislature and are funded by State money: the College of Agriculture and Life Sciences, the College of Human Ecology, and the School of Industrial and Labor Relations. So New York State residents attending any one of the three public ones are getting an education at an expensive private university at far more reasonable public prices. That is quite a bargain.

It is puzzling to us that more universities and states have not entered into such public–private partnerships. In fact, we once did a study for a state board of higher education that was interested in opening a new state institution in an underserved part of the state. Of all the options we tried out with citizens and state leaders, we thought that opening an innovative institution just like Cornell's public–private partnership was the best choice. (That state didn't do it—unfortunately.)

Proprietary Colleges

Many parents do not understand what proprietary colleges are. They think of proprietary colleges as the one-year or two-year schools for computer training and the like that New Yorkers see advertised on the subway. Or they think of them as places where you can "buy" a college diploma without really doing the academic work that other colleges require—"diploma mills," people say. But, in fact, proprietary institutions include four-year schools and even graduate schools. So let's look carefully at this category.

Public and private colleges are nonprofit organizations, whose first responsibility is to their students. A proprietary college is a profit-making organization, whose first responsibility is to its owners and stockholders. Proprietary colleges are in business to make money. Their business happens to be education. There is nothing wrong with that, but you should think about whether their motive to make money might color their decisions about the resources they put into the education they provide.

We do not mean to say that proprietary colleges provide a bad education; in fact, some provide a very good education. We did a study for one well-known multi-campus proprietary college and came away very impressed. It's probable that there is really a difference in quality between large proprietary institutions that have some history, like DeVry University, and some of the career and technical schools advertised in subway cars.

You should have a close look at any proprietary colleges your teenager is interested in. Check out their majors, their courses, their faculty, and their record of success. Remember that proprietary colleges are like private colleges when it comes to paying tuition. They are not cheap, and some do not have the scholarship funds that private and public colleges do. So check out the costs carefully, too.

[2]

Two-Year Colleges, Four-Year Colleges, and Universities

THIS CHAPTER EXPLAINS the differences in substance and atmosphere among two-year colleges, four-year colleges, and universities. Your teenager's own educational goals and future career choice as well as your family's financial situation will likely dictate which of these types of institutions makes the most sense for your teenager and your family. In conjunction with deciding on a public *vs.* private *vs.* proprietary college, your decision about a two-year college *vs.* a four-year college *vs.* a university might turn out to be the very first decision you have to make.

Two-Year Colleges

There are over 1,100 two-year colleges in the U.S. (that is a very big number indeed). Almost 1,000 of them are public colleges, usually referred to as "community colleges." Some two-year colleges might still carry the name of "junior college," which was more popular 100 years ago. Today, some two-year colleges have dropped the word "junior" or "community" from their names altogether—such as Montgomery College, a public two-year college in Montgomery County, Maryland, and Harcum College, a private two-year college in Bryn Mawr, Pennsylvania. So, again, remember that names of colleges can be tricky.

Some two-year colleges have one campus, while others have expanded to more than one campus, undoubtedly to be in easier reach of more prospective commuting students. Some two-year colleges operate independently, while others are part of a system—such as those operated by City Colleges of Chicago, with campuses spread across the city; those operated by Cuyahoga Community College, with campuses spread across Cuyahoga County (in and around Cleveland, Ohio); and those operated by the Maine Community Colleges System, with campuses spread across the state.

Public two-year colleges are funded by local (city or county) governments and/or state governments. As tuition continues to rise in colleges across the U.S., more and more students are considering attending a public two-year college first—before transferring to a four-year college to finish a degree. Because public two-year colleges have the lowest college tuition rates, this is a great strategy for saving family money for use later on at a more expensive public or private four-year college.

Although more and more high school students are choosing to start college at a two-year college, the average age of two-year college students is about 28 or 29. That is because many adults enrolling in college also choose two-year colleges. Some of those adults never attended college right after high school; others left college for a job or because of family responsibilities. Now they find themselves needing that college degree, and so they start college or return to college—usually part time, while working. For many of these adults, it is easier to get into a two-year college, and they can finish core courses or even earn a two-year degree there, before going on to a more expensive four-year college if they need or want a four-year degree.

So the atmosphere in two-year college classes, which are partly filled with adults who have chosen to be there to meet a goal that they have set for themselves, can be a bit more serious than the atmosphere in an 18-year-old's recent high school classes. Most two-year colleges are "commuter colleges"—that is, students do not live on campus in dorms, but rather commute to classes from their homes. Only about 25 percent of two-year colleges have dormitories. Because most adults are working while attending classes and many have family responsibilities to attend to, scheduling at a two-year college is more flexible, with weekend and evening classes being more available than at a typical liberal arts four-year college. All of these differences taken together can make the atmosphere on a two-year campus a bit different from the atmosphere at a traditional four-year college.

Interestingly, The City University of New York opened a new community college for the first time in many years in 2012—the Stella and Charles Guttman Community College. It is designed to offer a more supportive environment for its students, who are quite unlike most community college students. The average (median) age of Guttman students is just 19, and almost all of them attend full time. Smaller than many community colleges, Guttman offers degrees in just five majors and includes experiential learning and internships in its program. Though Guttman does not offer dormitory living for its students, Guttman students still probably have a more traditional college experience than students at most other two-year colleges have.

Two-year colleges award associate's degrees for two years' worth of completed courses, usually totaling about 60 credits. Calling them "two-year colleges" implies that students can complete their study there in two years. However, as we have already explained, the majority of two-year college students nationwide study just part time; thus, they can take three, four, or even more years to complete those 60 or so credits and earn an associate's degree.

The Path from Two-Year Colleges to Four-Year Colleges and Universities

Credits earned at a two-year college are supposed to be transferable to a four-year college or university. But some—or, perhaps, more like many—four-year colleges and universities will not accept all of the credits that students earn at two-year colleges. By the way, some four-year colleges and universities will not accept all of the credits that students earn at other four-year colleges or universities, either. This breakdown in the process of transferring earned credits from college to college is truly unfortunate for students and often seems unfair.

Most colleges set their own standards for what credits to accept and what credits to reject—unless it's a public college, and then the government might get involved. For example, some colleges won't accept credits for a course unless they themselves also offer the course. So if a student studies engineering technology at a two-year college and wants to transfer after one year to a four-college that does not teach engineering, that student might well lose some hard-earned credits. Even colleges within one system—say, a citywide system of public colleges—can be uncooperative when it comes to accepting each other's credits. So what should you do?

The best way to make sure that all of a student's two-year college credits transfer to a four-year college or university is for the student to earn an associate's degree. Why? Because more four-year colleges and universities will accept an associate's degree as a completed package (and, thus, all 60 or so of the credits that went into earning it) than will accept credits for individual courses not culminating in a degree.

One way to maximize your teenager's chances of transferring two-year credits to four-year institutions is to ask the two-year college of interest to your child about "articulation agreements." An articulation agreement is like a contract between two colleges, worked out in advance, that says that students can transfer their two-year college credits easily and perhaps also be accepted into given majors at the four-year college. Although articulation agreements can be difficult to locate and difficult to understand, they can be very useful. Make sure you ask as many questions as you need to.

Four-Year Colleges and Universities

Traditionally, only four-year colleges and universities could award bachelor's degrees. A bachelor's degree indicates a longer and more advanced level of college study than an associate's degree. A bachelor's degree is preferred by many employers, and it is required if a student wants to pursue a graduate or professional degree, like a master's degree or a doctoral degree in any field of study. Bachelor's degrees are generally worth about 120 credits, though some colleges in some majors might require a few more than that.

Just to keep things complicated, however, about 20 states now allow their public two-year community colleges to offer a limited number of bachelor's degrees, meaning that students will be staying at the community college a couple of years longer to earn more credits. Typically, the bachelor's degrees awarded by two-year colleges are in applied sciences and technical fields, especially where local employers are demanding workers trained in those fields, but no four-year college is providing the needed training. Because two-year and four-year public colleges are paid for with tax dollars, state legislatures are careful to avoid situations where many public institutions are offering the same thing in the same place— and, thus, taxpayers are unnecessarily double or triple paying for the same thing. Where public two-year colleges are allowed to offer bachelor's degrees, you can be sure that some talking has been done first with the public four-year colleges nearby.

If you and your teenager are thinking that a four-year college or university is the right option immediately upon high school graduation, then you have a choice of something like a couple thousand institutions in the U.S.—and more, of course, if you are also looking outside of the U.S. Your decision may be made easier if you have already decided whether that institution should be public or private, as explained in the previous chapter. However, if financing your teenager's education is not your top concern, then you have many, many, many public and private colleges to choose from, and you may well end up with both public and private options on your list. As you probably already know, four-year colleges and universities come in all shapes and sizes, and we are going to talk about a wide range of them in the coming chapters.

How does a university differ from a four-year college? A university is usually a larger institution with more students and more professors than a two-year college or a four-year college. A university offers both undergraduate and graduate degrees. (Undergraduate degrees are associate's and bachelor's degrees; graduate degrees are master's and doctoral degrees.) As usual in this complicated world of college, some four-year colleges also offer graduate degrees, but the degree fields are more likely limited in number.

A large university is usually made up of more than one "school" or "college," each of which is focused on a different field of study. One of these schools or colleges typically focuses on the liberal arts (more about that in the next chapter); others might focus on specific academic or career fields, like education, engineering, fine arts, business, or health sciences. Because students are studying in so many different fields in various schools or colleges of the university, it is likely that there is a more diverse student body on a university campus than, say, on a small liberal arts college campus. For some students, living in that kind of setting is stimulating and rewarding; for others, it is overwhelming. How comfortable would your teenager be navigating in a university setting?

One thought about the application process: Some universities let their own schools and/or colleges make different demands at application time. For example, some might require additional essays, additional college admission test scores, portfolios of student work, or auditions. If your teenager is considering applying to a university, make sure that you check out the application process carefully—that is, check the application requirements of the university's specific school or college your teenager is interested in. Also check to see whether a student is permitted to apply to more than one school or college within the university; some universities allow that, and others don't.

Universities usually award different types of four-year bachelor's degrees, depending on a student's major field of study, such as a Bachelor of Arts, Bachelor of Science, Bachelor of Architecture, Bachelor of Business Administration, Bachelor of Fine Arts (in dance, visual art, or music, although some offer a Bachelor of Music degree), and more. Some universities offer two-year associate's degrees to students on their way to a four-year bachelor's degree—though there is nothing to stop a student at one of those universities from leaving with just an associate's degree in hand.

Sometimes the schools or colleges within a university are only for graduate students who have already earned a four-year bachelor's degree. Graduate students might attend a university's medical school, law school, school of theology, journalism school, or others. A university awards master's degrees and sometimes doctoral degrees to graduate students. It is typical for a university to offer bachelor's degrees in more subject fields than master's degrees and to offer master's degrees in more subject fields than doctoral degrees. Because universities offer graduate degrees in graduate programs, they typically have professors and advanced students doing more research on campus than two-year and four-year colleges do. The point of graduate study is, in fact, to create new knowledge, which comes out of research.

That's a lot to take in. Nonetheless, there is a higher education institution—and undoubtedly more than one—that is the right fit for your teenager. It might be a two-year college, a four-year college, or a university. Or it might be a two-year college first, followed by a four-year college or university. Your decision on this topic will determine a lot about what your teenager gets out of the college experience.

[3]
Liberal Arts Study and Technical Study

THIS CHAPTER LOOKS AT the choice of liberal arts study *vs.* technical study—regardless of the type of higher education institution the student attends—and what effect that choice will have both immediately on the student's college courses and later on how the student might be viewed by future employers.

Why Liberal Arts Study?

A study of the "liberal arts" means that students take courses in a variety of academic subjects, typically including literature, history, mathematics, fine arts, philosophy, biological and/or physical sciences, foreign languages, and one or more of the social sciences, like psychology, sociology, and anthropology. Sometimes these subjects as a group are also called the "arts and sciences" or "humanities and sciences."

A "liberal arts college" usually refers to a relatively small, private, four-year college, where a student studies the subject fields that make up the liberal arts and chooses to major in one of them. A university, as we have said earlier, typically has one school or college within it that is devoted to the "liberal arts," or the "liberal arts and sciences," or the "arts and sciences," or whatever that university's favorite version of the name is.

A classical liberal arts education is an idea from centuries ago—indeed an idea dating back to the glory days of Greece and Rome. Today, some people believe that studying the liberal arts is old-fashioned and does not prepare a student for the real world. Their reasoning is that a liberal arts student spends his or her time studying across too many subjects, some of which do not seem to have a clear and immediate connection to a future career and which, as a group, leave the liberal arts student without focus. However, others believe that learning to think critically and creatively and learning to write logically and analytically across a variety of subject fields make a student flexible so that he or she is able to handle the complex problems that come up in the real world. They believe that a liberal arts student's ability to apply his or her broad range of knowledge and skills to new problems is the most important thing, even if the student is not highly trained in any one technical or career field. They believe that, even in a tough economic climate, employers will want new employees who are well rounded in their studies and who can adapt what they have learned to the new situations they will face in the workplace.

To be sure, almost all liberal arts students do major in one subject field—biology, French, sociology, mathematics, English literature, political science, art history, or one of many, many more fields. So they do gain in-depth knowledge of one field as they gain an understanding of many other fields; it's just that the one field in which they major is less likely to put them on a particular career path immediately upon graduation.

Some people believe that one advantage to liberal arts study is that such students typically have to meet distribution requirements (sometimes called "general education" requirements) during their four years, but usually concentrated in the first year or two. This means that students are required to take courses across perhaps four or five or so academic areas in order to make sure that they come away with a broad intellectual background and that they have sampled a variety of academic fields before they choose to major in one field. For example, students might be required to take one or more courses in the social sciences, in languages and literature, in the natural sciences and mathematics, in the fine arts, and so on, depending on the college. One important advantage to having distribution requirements is that it causes students to look into whole academic fields that are rarely taught in high schools—like anthropology or sociology or art history or linguistics. Without distribution requirements, many students would never take a look at some of these disciplines and would never know what they had missed.

Some colleges go one step further and require certain courses of all students—the actual courses, not just the subject fields. So, instead of saying to students that they must take two courses in the social sciences, for example, the college will specify that all students must take Sociology 101 and Psychology 101. In those cases, the college has decided which courses its professors feel are most fundamental to developing the foundation for more advanced college study and to developing a broad understanding of and ability to engage in the modern world. Because all students have taken these same required core courses, professors can use that shared knowledge to make connections across subject fields every year from then on, thus helping students begin to think about issues from a variety of perspectives.

One note of clarification: Degrees that are simply in the liberal arts (e.g., a B.A. in Liberal Studies, an A.S. in the Liberal Arts and Sciences) rather than in a specific subject field major are a different story. Some two-year colleges use this type of A.A. or A.S. associate's degree to indicate that students have taken a broad range of subjects (with an A.S. degree usually indicating more science and/or mathematics requirements) and that they are now prepared to continue into a bachelor's degree program at a four-year college; essentially, students' two years of liberal arts distribution requirements have been completed at the two-year college in advance of choosing a major. When four-year colleges award students a bachelor's degree in liberal arts rather than in a specific subject field, it is sometimes because those students zigzagged their way through college (or were adults returning to college), changing their minds about their majors too often to accumulate enough credits to meet the requirements in any one subject field, and it is sometimes because an innovative college has decided not to have majors at all. Not every four-year college will award a degree in the "liberal arts," without naming a major.

Why Technical Study?

Technical study usually focuses on one or more specific career fields, such as engineering, computer studies, construction management, fashion design, health services, and more. Like liberal arts study, technical study can be done at proprietary colleges, two-year colleges, and four-year colleges or universities. Two of our nation's best universities specialize in technical study—the Massachusetts Institute of Technology (commonly referred to as MIT) and the California Institute of Technology (commonly referred to as Caltech). While some people might look down on technical study generally as being intellectually inferior to the liberal arts tradition, everyone has to admit that there are really no better universities in the U.S. than MIT and Caltech.

A "technical college" used to refer to a two-year college offering associate's degrees in specific career fields. Now there are many four-year technical colleges as well. Some technical colleges require students to take some liberal arts courses; others do not. Some technical colleges even offer a two-year degree in liberal arts—undoubtedly because some students just have not made a career decision yet.

To take one example, The City University of New York's New York City College of Technology (commonly referred to as City Tech) is a four-year technical college (although it did, in fact, start as a two-year college). City Tech offers a range of both associate's and bachelor's degrees, including a B.Tech. (Bachelor of Technology) in certain technical fields. Interestingly enough, in the liberal arts, City Tech offers an A.A. and an A.S. (where the A.S. requires more science and math study) for students who are just not ready as freshmen or sophomores to make a decision to study in one technical career field; both of these degrees are reasonable ones for students to take if they are planning to transfer directly to a four-year college and choose a major field there.

Looking statewide in New York for some other examples, the State University of New York has a variety of general technical colleges and some very appealing technical colleges in specific fields. They include the College of Technology at Canton, College of Agriculture and Technology at Cobleskill, College of Technology at Delhi, College of Environmental Science and Forestry, Fashion Institute of Technology, Maritime College, and SUNY Polytechnic Institute.

Technical study at the college level usually works best for students who leave high school knowing that they want to study in a specific technical field. So, if your teenager knows that he or she wants to be an engineer, or an architect, or a fashion designer, for example, and has been consistent over several years in that goal, then technical study can be a good choice. It will move your teenager through the exact right courses on a clear path and on toward a marketable set of skills as efficiently as possible—and moving students through college efficiently is one great way to save money.

One of the challenges of pursuing study at a technical college is that, not surprisingly, teenagers change their minds a lot. What is interesting this month might not be interesting next month. Because many technical programs have many required courses, which are often carefully sequenced, it is difficult when a student changes his or her mind after a semester or a year or even two years. Undoubtedly, courses that a student took as an electrical engineering technology major will not transfer well to an accounting major, and common sense will tell you why.

It could be even worse if a student wants to transfer from a medical technology major at a technology college to a liberal arts field at a four-year college. As we said earlier, some colleges will not give any credit for courses that a student took at another college if they themselves don't offer those courses. So, there will be liberal arts colleges that will not give credit for any medical technology courses—no matter how hard they were or how well the student did. To make it worse, such a student might have to catch up on liberal arts distribution requirements that the new college's own students took as freshmen. After both losing some technical credits and having to make up liberal arts credits, some students could find themselves a full year—or more—behind.

One thing that might help students get it right the first time is to put them into high school activities that expose them to careers. In high schools we have worked with, students are given the chance to do job shadowing at work sites or go on career exploration field trips or—if they are motivated and hard-working—do an internship in the real world. We believe strongly in the value of internships and have talked about them often in our podcast; the high school we co-founded was started in partnership with the National Academy Foundation, whose multi-faceted program has a wise and strong emphasis on internships in career fields for high school students.

We have seen far too many high school students simply not participate in these kinds of work-related activities when they are offered. That is a huge mistake. This is how your teenager can find out firsthand what it is like to be on a construction site or in a financial services office or in a law office or in a veterinary clinic or in a retail shop or in a thousand other places we have seen offered to students. Nothing substitutes for this kind of real-world experience—and it's free to you. Sometimes your teenager is even paid for an internship. So make sure your teenager takes advantage of everything that is offered in high school when it comes to exploring the world of work.

One last warning: Be careful that your teenager is planning to major in something he or she really wants and not just in something you want. You can force a child to do something for a couple of years of college—and some especially strong-willed parents can even get a child to go on to law school when that child has no interest in the law (we could tell you a lot of real stories like that)—but eventually your control will run out. College life and then work life are hard enough when you are passionate about what you are doing. How must they be for students and then young employees when they do not like what they are doing? If at all possible, try to support what your teenager's interests are—even if those interests do not look like the best way to earn a dollar in the job market right away. Because having a student go through switching majors because he or she isn't happy in any one of them is costly, and having a student do something he or she loves is priceless, as they say.

Choosing Between Liberal Arts Study and Technical Study

Some people believe that all students should start out in the liberal arts so that they have a well-rounded education and so that they can sample many fields of study—including those that are not available to most high school students—before settling in on one.

Some people believe that students who are committed to a specific career field when they leave high school should be able to pursue it immediately in college and thus move into that career faster, saving both time and money.

Keep in mind that either liberal arts study or technical study can be pursued at both two-year and four-year, both public and private institutions, depending on your teenager's qualifications and your family's circumstances. So the whole range of college options remains open.

In the interest of full disclosure, both of us took the liberal arts route in our undergraduate degrees—one in English literature and one in sociology—and it is possible that we are a bit biased in favor of having a liberal arts base. In Marie's case, she never would have known that the field of sociology existed had it not been for the distribution requirements mandated by her traditional liberal arts college, Barnard. And all three of Regina's children were gently guided—both by their parents and by their colleges—into getting a liberal arts grounding first, before they went on to study for quite specialized bachelor's degrees (in music performance, in visual arts and media, and in dance). Not one of us regrets the choice.

[4]
Colleges with Specific Missions

THIS CHAPTER LOOKS AT groups of colleges, each of which was founded with a specific mission in mind. Some groups are categorized by the student population they were established to serve, others by the special or unique academic programs they offer, and some by both. Some parents and students never consider whole groups of colleges because they don't know much about them. Yet, it is possible that one of these groups would be attractive—even life changing—for your teenager.

Historically Black Colleges and Universities

Commonly referred to as HBCUs, historically black colleges and universities were established with the mission of educating African-American students solely or primarily. The just over 100 HBCUs can be found in many states and in both rural and urban areas.

They are public and private, large and small (even very small), two-year and four-year colleges, and some have graduate schools. Some offer liberal arts degrees, some offer technical degrees, and some offer both.

HBCUs were founded to serve students who had been excluded from many other higher education institutions because of their race. The three earliest HBCUs were founded in Pennsylvania and Ohio before the Civil War, but many were founded in the South shortly after the Civil War. Those Southern HBCUs share a proud tradition of becoming the first collegiate homes of family members of freed slaves.

Some HBCUs have produced great black leaders—like Booker T. Washington, who attended Hampton University, and like Thurgood Marshall, who attended both Lincoln University and Howard University School of Law. Some have put great black leaders from many walks of life on their payrolls as professors and administrators—like Fisk University, where Charles Spurgeon Johnson, the intellectual architect of the Harlem Renaissance, served as Fisk's first black president and where Harlem Renaissance writers and artists, like Arna Bontemps, James Weldon Johnson, and Aaron Douglas all worked.

Today, HBCUs enroll students who are not black—just as historically white colleges and universities now enroll students who are not white. Some observers say that it has become harder for HBCUs to recruit African-American students now that they are welcome at both selective and nonselective colleges across the U.S. That is probably true to some degree. Nonetheless, there is still a strong sense of community among the alumni/alumnae of HBCUs and a strong sense of tradition on HBCU campuses. For some

African-American students especially, that could be a good fit for what they are looking for in a college, and a shared culture could go a long way toward helping them feel comfortable on a college campus, especially if it is far from home.

You can find a complete listing of HBCUs on the website of the White House Initiative on Historically Black Colleges and Universities.

Hispanic-Serving Institutions

There are over 250 colleges and universities that have been designated during the past 50 years as Hispanic-serving institutions (HSIs), meaning that they have a student enrollment that is at least 25 percent Hispanic. They are located in states across the U.S. from California to Massachusetts and from Washington to Florida. Some HSIs are large public universities, some are large public community colleges, and some are small private liberal arts colleges. Many HSIs receive federal funds to support programs and scholarships that are designed to help low-income Hispanic students succeed in college.

Although HSIs do not have the same kind of historical traditions that HBCUs have—perhaps because they were not founded originally with a mission to serve Hispanic students—they do offer an environment where Hispanic students might more easily find classmates with a similar cultural background. First-generation Hispanic college students—that is, students whose parents did not attend college—might find it easier to fit into this supportive college environment, thus improving their chances of long-term success.

The Hispanic Association of Colleges and Universities maintains a list of member institutions.

Single-Sex Colleges and Universities

Colleges and universities that were started in America's earliest days were all institutions for men. They were all single-sex institutions then.

Seven of the eight well-known Ivy League institutions served only male students when they were founded in the 1600s and 1700s: the University of Pennsylvania, Columbia, Dartmouth, Brown, Princeton, Harvard, and Yale. Among the Ivies, only Cornell, the youngest of the Ivies, was founded as a co-educational university, which took as its mission from its first day to enroll both men and women.

As time went on, many Ivies created a "sister" school for women: the University of Pennsylvania had its College for Women, Columbia had Barnard, Brown had Pembroke, and Harvard had Radcliffe. Of these, only Barnard remains.

The tradition of single-sex colleges is particularly strong in the Northeast, perhaps because that is where so many of our country's oldest higher education institutions are located. In addition to Barnard, women's colleges in the Northeast include Bryn Mawr College, Mount Holyoke College, Simmons College, Smith College, and Wellesley College. But there are well-known women's colleges located in other regions of the U.S. as well—like Mills College and Scripps College in California, Stephens College in Missouri, Hollins University and Mary Baldwin College in Virginia, Saint Mary's College (the sister school of the University of Notre Dame) in Indiana, and Agnes Scott College and Spelman College in Georgia. Spelman has the distinction of also being an excellent HBCU.

Interestingly and for whatever reason (probably rooted in financial issues), some of these women's colleges now allow men to enroll in their graduate programs only, thus maintaining the traditional women's college atmosphere for their undergraduate residential students. Today, there are just over 40 women's colleges in the U.S.

Oddly, only a handful of men's colleges remain, perhaps partly because now there are actually more women than men going to college. The men's college you have most likely heard of is Morehouse College, which is an academically rigorous HBCU located in Georgia and which is the men's counterpart to Spelman. Morehouse has a roster of famous alumni, ranging from Martin Luther King, Jr., to Samuel L. Jackson and Spike Lee. Here are two more appealing men's colleges: Hampden-Sydney College, which was founded in 1775 in Virginia and has a long and fascinating history (Patrick Henry and James Madison were among its first Trustees); and Wabash College, which is located in Indiana and was cited in the book *Colleges That Change Lives* as an institution that is successful in creating engaged students, who become leaders in their chosen fields.

While most single-sex institutions have opened their doors to the opposite sex over the years and especially in the past 50 years, those that remain carry on a tradition that their graduates wholeheartedly support. Some of their graduates—and indeed their families—believe that students can focus better on their studies when they are not being distracted by social interactions with the opposite sex in the classroom. Some of their graduates believe that students will develop a stronger sense of community and camaraderie with their classmates in single-sex institutions. Some of their graduates appreciate the histories and philosophies of these institutions—especially perhaps graduates of women's colleges who feel that they are better supported as young women and are encouraged to set and pursue whatever education and career goals they can imagine for themselves.

You can search for women's colleges on the Women's College Coalition website.

Colleges and Universities with Selected Academic Specialties

Regardless of the wide range of subjects most students study in high school, for some students one particular subject is the only reason to come to school. That is one reason that it is so important for high schools to offer a full array of subjects and a broad schedule of after-school activities. We all want each child to be able to find something he or she can be passionate about learning.

Students who find that thing they are passionate about in high school—whether it is art or biology or writing or music or social justice issues or robotics or theater or Spanish or something else—could indeed be ready to specialize when they start college. What those students have to decide is whether to attend a university—which offers the field of study they are interested in, along with many, many others—or a college that is entirely dedicated to the field of study they are interested in.

What are the pros and cons of choosing a university or an independent dedicated college? On one hand, a student who does really well in one field and does not want to spend time studying others might progress quicker, learn more in depth, and be better focused in a college that is dedicated to that field. On the other hand, a student who ends up wanting to change to a different field of study might have an easier time doing so in a university setting, where that student could end up in an entirely different part of the university. Of course, some universities make those kinds of transfers easy, and some make them quite difficult. In some universities, it is difficult even to take a course in a different part of the university, much less transfer to it.

As a parent, you need to understand what your teenager is getting into and whether he or she has been prepared for it. Has your teenager gotten good instruction in high school in his or her field of interest? Has your teenager gotten training outside of school if that is expected (especially in the arts)? Has your teenager seen what studying that field on a college campus might be like? Has your teenager had a chance to shadow someone working in that field or, better still, had a chance to have an internship in that field? If not, has your teenager had a chance to talk with someone who works in that field to see what that work life is like?

We find that many students' ideas of what certain college majors are like and what certain career fields are like are simply not based in reality. If you are going to let your teenager choose a specialized college or specialized school within a university, make sure that the two of you have done some homework first. Check out the specialized college or the specialized school within a university carefully, looking particularly at what it might be like if your teenager changes his or her mind—because that does happen.

THE ARTS. So, if you are convinced that specializing is the right thing for your teenager, let's look at the arts first. Students at specialized colleges and university schools for the arts are really good at what they do. They are talented to begin with, and they are committed. They have likely practiced hard for years—whether in vocal music or instrumental music or visual arts or dance. They have studied their art in school and outside of school, most likely in private lessons over many years. They prepared an audition piece or portfolio and then presented it to a panel of judges. Once accepted, they knew they would have to continue to practice and work hard almost every day. They knew that the competition to get into the college was fierce, and they knew that the competition would continue to be fierce among their classmates once they were in. As hard as all that sounds, there are many high school seniors every year who meet all of these standards and excel at their craft; they are going to specialized arts institutions.

Students who are passionate about the arts have quite a number of well-regarded choices. Some schools devoted to the arts are within larger institutions, including the Eastman School of Music at the University of Rochester, the Tisch School of the Arts at New York University, the Conservatory of Music at Oberlin College, the Meadows School of the Arts at Southern Methodist University, and the Jacobs School of Music at Indiana University.

Turning to institutions wholly dedicated to the arts, there is the highly selective Juilliard School in New York City, well known for its degrees in drama, music, and dance. The School of the Art Institute of Chicago, associated with the famous art museum of the same name, offers degrees in studio art, but also in art history and art education as well as other arts-related specialties.

Founded in 1887, Pratt Institute in New York City offers both undergraduate and graduate degrees, with 22 associate's and bachelor's degrees in the arts and arts-related fields, including degrees in architecture, graphic design, painting and drawing, illustration, film, photography, digital arts, fashion, interior design, and art history. Rhode Island School of Design (commonly known as RISD—pronounced RIZ-dee) offers 15 Bachelors of Fine Arts majors in visual arts and design specialties and a Bachelor of Architecture degree. Sometimes we forget that architecture is indeed one of the arts.

Berklee College of Music in Boston, which is dedicated to the study of music, is a bit different from most other music schools because it draws students from around the world to study contemporary, rather than classical, music. It offers degrees in a wide range of music specialties, including performance, composition, film scoring, music therapy, music education, production and engineering, and music business. Although all students at Berklee can play an instrument or sing extraordinarily well, not all Berklee students major in performance. But even performance majors take courses that require them to use their heads rather than their hands or voices; they study music theory and music history, for example, because music is an academic discipline just like any other. Berklee's new graduate campus in Valencia, Spain—again, dedicated to the study of music—offers its master's degrees programs in breathtaking facilities, designed by modern architect Santiago Calatrava, in a setting that truly showcases global music.

New York City is home to Fordham University's Lincoln Center campus in the heart of Manhattan. Fordham offers a unique joint dance program with The Ailey School, the school of the Alvin Ailey American Dance Theater, located just blocks away. Students must apply to and audition for the Ailey program as well as apply to Fordham and be accepted by both. Students take a core set of liberal arts courses at Fordham, with strict distribution requirements; spend perhaps 15 to 20 hours per week in a rigorous set of classical and contemporary dance classes at Ailey; take academic courses at Ailey, such as dance history and music for dancers; and participate in the additional rehearsals and performances that are part of all dancers' lives. Students graduate with a Bachelor of Fine Arts (B.F.A.) in Dance.

ENGINEERING. Let's look at a quite different field of study. Students who are intrigued by the rigorous technical field of engineering might consider a school of engineering within a large university (many big public universities have them and quite a few private universities also have them), like the Massachusetts Institute of Technology, California Institute of Technology, University of Texas, Texas A & M University, University of Illinois, University of Southern California, Carnegie Mellon University, Cornell University, Columbia University, and many more. Engineering programs are often part of a large university because engineering courses are expensive to run, given the equipment and materials that are needed.

But, some smaller colleges have engineering programs as well. Take the example of Manhattan College (a private Catholic college in the Bronx in New York City), which has 3,500 students, but offers a School of Engineering with both undergraduate and graduate degrees. Or the impressive Harvey Mudd College (one of The Claremont Colleges in California) with just 800 undergraduate students. This small-campus atmosphere might be better for your teenager than one of the large public or private universities with schools of engineering.

Or students interested in engineering might consider an institution that is dedicated to the study of engineering (and related fields), like the Milwaukee School of Engineering or the Colorado School of Mines.

Just remember that students might be required to take some liberal arts courses early on in an engineering program to provide some humanities balance to the heavy load of mathematics and sciences that engineering students take. The Fu Foundation School of Engineering and Applied Science at Columbia University has this impressive and perhaps surprising statement on its website:

> *Engineering has been called the newest liberal art. At Columbia Engineering, students not only study science and mathematics and gain technical skills but also study literature, philosophy, art history, music theory, and major civilizations through the Core Curriculum in the humanities.*

> *Students are encouraged to consider the wide range of possibilities open to them, both academically and professionally. To this end, the first and second years of the four-year undergraduate program comprise approximately 66 semester points of credit that expose students to a cross-fertilization of ideas from different disciplines within the University. The sequence of study proceeds from an engagement with engineering and scientific fundamentals, along with humanities and social sciences, toward an increasingly focused training in the third and fourth years designed to give students mastery of certain principles and arts central to engineering and applied science.*

The brilliance of this position comes in the notion that students who find that engineering is not what they had expected—for whatever reason—are well equipped to transfer to another field of study and move many of these core credits with them. For some engineering students, these liberal arts courses could be a drag; for other engineering students, they could turn out to save the day.

BUSINESS. Students who have decided that business is their future can attend business schools that can be found at many public and private universities—some popular for their undergraduate business schools and some for their graduate business schools—including the University of Pennsylvania, Harvard University, University of Chicago, Stanford University, New York University, Northwestern University, University of Michigan at Ann Arbor, University of Virginia, and many more.

Stand-alone institutions dedicated to the study of business are the other way to go. Students could consider higher education institutions like Babson College and Bentley University, both private colleges located in Massachusetts.

Military Service Academies

A different kind of academic specialty and career preparation is represented by our nation's five highly respected military service academies, which train officers for the military and provide an excellent collegiate education in selected academic fields as well: the United States Naval Academy in Maryland (commonly referred to as Annapolis), the United States Military Academy in New York (commonly referred to as West Point), the United States Air Force Academy in Colorado, the United States Coast Guard Academy in Connecticut, and the United States Merchant Marine Academy in New York.

Admission to the service academies is highly selective. Students interested in attending should be particularly good in mathematics and the sciences, because those subjects are the basis of much of the academic work at the service academies as well as the work that students will do upon graduating. The curriculum is really the best job training possible in these fields.

While there is no tuition, thus making this first-rate education an incredible bargain, there is a military service obligation of a number of years upon graduation. With that obligation, however, comes an officer's salary. So that is an attractive economic incentive for motivated students. Of course, in these turbulent times worldwide, the service obligation is something for families to consider carefully.

Just as with the HBCUs and single-sex institutions, there is a connectedness and pride that the students and graduates of the service academies feel and, indeed, live by. There are many alumni/alumnae in civilian life as well (after finishing their time in the military), who form a social and career network for service academy graduates for the rest of their lives.

If your teenager is smart and interested in military service, then the service academies are a great choice and will allow your teenager to enter the military as an officer. If you feel your teenager is likely to change his or her mind, then he or she is not ready to make the serious commitment to this course of study and way of life that would be required.

Faith-Based Colleges and Universities

"Faith-based"—that is, religious—colleges and universities are a broader category than you might think. They range from hundreds of small Bible colleges, which are dedicated to religious life and the study of religion, to very large universities that offer all fields of study, though with an underlying religious or moral or service-to-others orientation. In addition, there are theological seminaries, which are typically graduate schools and are designed mainly for individuals wishing to become ministers.

Some faith-based institutions require more religious study than others. Some require students to take just a couple of courses in theology or even philosophy, while others wrap their whole curriculum around their religious beliefs. Some require students to attend chapel services; some do not. Consequently, students who are not of the same faith as a college's founding religion might or might not be comfortable enrolling.

More U.S. colleges and universities than you might think have been founded by religious denominations; some of them retain their denomination affiliation, and some do not. In the U. S., most faith-based institutions are Jewish or Christian (including Catholic, African Methodist Episcopal, Baptist, Presbyterian, Methodist, Lutheran, and more).

Perhaps the two best-known Jewish universities in the U.S. are in the Northeast: Yeshiva University in New York City, which combines an academic and religious education; and Brandeis University, which is a nonsectarian Jewish-supported institution located outside Boston.

Understanding the world of some 200 Catholic colleges and universities in the U.S. is complicated by the fact that they have been founded by various orders (including the Jesuits, Dominicans, Lasallians, and Franciscans) and by other groups within the Catholic community. Well-known and respected Catholic institutions include the University of Notre Dame, Georgetown University, Boston College, Fordham University, Villanova University, and the College of the Holy Cross. Some Catholic higher education institutions sound as though they might be public because of their names, like the University of Dallas, Manhattan College, Saint Louis University, Santa Clara University, and the University of San

Diego.

To be sure, many students who attend Catholic colleges and universities, especially the best-known ones, are not Catholic. We wonder how many parents know anything about their traditions. Here is Regina's viewpoint about sending her daughter to a Jesuit university:

I was attending my daughter Polly's welcome assembly at Fordham, where she was starting the joint Alvin Ailey/Fordham B.F.A. in Dance program. I sent Polly to Fordham for its dance program (one of the best in the country), but I got a lot more than I expected. Not being Catholic, I knew relatively little about the Jesuits and their almost 500-year history, except that I had always heard that Jesuit schools had a reputation for academic excellence. At that time in 2011, Father Joseph McShane was president of Fordham (and, fortunately, still is at the time of this publication), and he spoke to the incoming freshmen and their parents. Now, I have been in large and small meetings with quite a few college presidents, but Father McShane was one of the very best I had ever heard. He explained to us what a Jesuit education was, something I am embarrassed to admit that I knew virtually nothing about. He said that Fordham students were taught to wrestle with important moral and ethical issues, to care for others, to despair over injustice, and to give back to their communities. I never looked back. Polly, my dancer, ended up with as broad and deep a liberal arts education as I could have hoped for, thanks to Father McShane and the Jesuits.

The point of this personal story is not that I am pushing a Jesuit education—though, clearly, I am impressed by what I witnessed over four years. The point is that you don't know what you don't know, and you have to find out, if you don't want your child to miss an opportunity you don't even know exists.

The list of colleges affiliated with or founded by Christian Protestant denominations is very long indeed and dates back to the beginning of our country. If you are interested, you can easily find lists of these colleges online by searching for "Methodist colleges," "Presbyterian colleges," "Baptist colleges," and so on. Some of these colleges are associated with the founding denomination mainly through historical traditions, and others are still actively affiliated today.

To find out how influential religion is in everyday life at a college, you will need to read online about the college's academic offerings and student life or, better still, call and ask or go visit and observe. For example, Baylor University describes itself on its website as "a private Christian university and a nationally ranked research institution," which was "chartered in 1845 by the Republic of Texas through the efforts of Baptist pioneers." Clearly, Baylor is saying that Christian values were and are a part of campus life. On the other hand, American University, Southern Methodist University, and Duke University all had early Methodist affiliations, but they are not considered faith-based institutions today, as you can tell by reading their websites.

Let's also look at the three Brigham Young University (BYU) campuses (in Utah, Idaho, and Hawai'i) that are part of the Church Educational System of The Church of Jesus Christ of Latter-day Saints. Faith is very much a part of everyday life on these campuses. Here is a statement from the BYU (Utah) website:

> *Initiated by students in 1949, the Honor Code emphasizes being honest, living a chaste and virtuous life, abstaining from alcohol and tobacco, using clean language and following other values encompassed in the doctrines of the Church of Jesus Christ. The code is supplemented by additional guidelines on dress, grooming and housing.*

Turning to the curriculum, there are four required religion courses at each BYU campus, including one on the Church's Book of Mormon. As part of the admissions process, applicants need to obtain an endorsement from a Church leader; if your family is not Mormon, your teenager would be interviewed by a Church bishop. So, while applying and attending could be a bit uncomfortable for students who are not Mormon (about 99 percent of students at BYU in Utah are, in fact, Mormons), tuition is remarkably low and the education is likely very good.

In our experience, faith-based institutions are usually quite up front about what they are all about. They are not trying to trick your teenager into going there, because that wouldn't be good for you or for them. Sometimes a college application will give you a clue by asking for your religion and the name and address of your church. Some ask for a recommendation from a minister. Many have a statement of their religious beliefs on their website or in their student handbook; you can read it and see whether your family supports it. So make sure you do your research.

Colleges and Universities for Students with Special Needs

While students with special needs can succeed at a wide variety of colleges and universities and while there are colleges and universities that have specific programs for special needs students, there are also a handful that are dedicated to serving them. Let's look at a few.

Gallaudet University in Washington, D.C., was established as a college by an Act of Congress in 1864 to serve deaf and hard-of-hearing students. It was then and still is the world's only such institution. The President of the United States signed the first diplomas of graduates in 1869 (by the way, that was Ulysses S. Grant), and that is a tradition that continues to this day. Perhaps surprisingly, up to 5 percent of the seats in each incoming undergraduate class are open to hearing students. Those seats are likely sought after by students who have a career interest in working with deaf children and adults in many different ways. Gallaudet's more than 1,700 students are pursuing both undergraduate and graduate degrees in what Gallaudet itself describes on its website as a "bilingual, diverse, multicultural institution"—with "bilingual" defined as American Sign Language and English. As an added bonus, Gallaudet's tuition is remarkably reasonable at about $14,000 a year because it is actually a public college (in this unusual case, funded by the federal government).

In upstate New York at the Rochester Institute of Technology, students can find the National Technical Institute for the Deaf, one of nine colleges of RIT. Established by an Act of Congress in 1965, NTID is the world's first and largest technology-focused college for students who are deaf or hard of hearing. NTID offers career-oriented associate's degrees in technical fields and associate's degrees that lead directly into bachelor's degree study at RIT's other colleges. NTID also offers the support services that deaf and hard-of-hearing students would need in order to study in the other RIT colleges. Because it is a public college, even though it is within a private university, the tuition is quite reasonable.

Let's look at a college for students with different needs: Landmark College in Vermont, founded in 1985 to help students with dyslexia succeed in college. Offering several associate's degrees, a Bachelor of Arts in Liberal Studies, a brand-new Bachelor of Arts in Studio Art, and a brand-new Bachelor of Science in Computer Science, Landmark now serves a variety of students who learn differently—that is, students with learning disabilities, autism spectrum disorder, and attention deficit hyperactivity disorder. Landmark provides an impressive array of academic and personal support services to help its students cope with college courses and college life. Summer programs are also available to rising high school juniors and seniors who learn differently and could benefit from Landmark's approach; that could be a great head start for special needs high school students, regardless of whether they go on to attend Landmark for college.

Some students with special needs feel isolated or left out in an educational setting that is filled with all kinds of students and would prefer a school that focused on them, where they feel they could fit into a community of students they could easily relate to. For such students, a college like Gallaudet or Landmark can be an empowering, even life-changing, experience.

However, other students with special needs prefer to be mainstreamed into an educational setting full of all types of students, where they can have the full range of friends and classmates and where they can learn how to adapt to the kinds of environments they might meet in their everyday lives and in the world of work. Parents of such students will want to make sure that they are supported in their college lives by the services they will need. While all colleges are supposed to provide such services, the fact is that they do so to very different degrees (just as public schools, which are required by federal law to provide a range of educational and support services to students with special needs, do so, unfortunately, to very different degrees).

So, parents, check out the office for student support services (sometimes known as the office for disability services) at the colleges your teenager is interested in attending. Talk to a staff member in the office and try to gauge how approachable the staff members are. See what the office provides: counseling, tutoring in academic subjects, testing accommodations, interpreters (in American Sign Language), notetakers to attend classes with your teenager, and "assistive technologies," which include a range of devices that can make it easier for your teenager to function in the classroom or at home (like a pen that also records an audio version of the class lecture). To be sure, you should have had many of these services available in high school, if your teenager attended a public high school that took its charge of providing for students with IEPs seriously. But regardless of your high school experience, you can and should expect such services for your teenager as he or she starts college.

One other and incredibly useful thing offices of student support services do is to help students become advocates for themselves. They help students learn how to talk to their professors about what accommodations they need to be successful in class and how to seek out help from other offices if they need it. In other words, they help students learn how to cope in ways that will be valuable to them throughout their lives.

One last critical point for parents of students with special needs: You must provide the college your teenager chooses with an up-to-date evaluation of his or her case, including a diagnosis. These evaluations can be done in public high schools by school or school district staff. However, if you have not had a good relationship in the past with these school staff members (who are often overworked, which can sometimes lead to underperformance in preparing these evaluations), then get the evaluation done privately. While that can be expensive, a thorough evaluation could be the difference between college success and failure for your teenager.

Colleges Offering Online Study

Online study is becoming increasingly popular, with complete degrees now being offered through online study, especially at the graduate level. Even if a fully online degree is not attractive, many individual courses are now offered partly online and partly in class ("hybrid courses") or completely online so that students do not have to attend as many classes or any classes on the campus.

For some students, an online course or even an online degree can be handy and can enable students to earn credits when they cannot travel to a college campus. But online courses require a lot of self-discipline, which makes it difficult for some students to get good grades—but, more important than just the grade, makes it difficult for some students to learn the material and remember it so they can use it in future courses or on the job.

Online courses are not easier than regular courses. They require just as much work from students, often with less guidance from the professor. Although most of our students had some experience with a high school online course in the high school we co-founded, we hesitated to put any of them in online college courses when they made the transition to our Early College partner—even though we knew we would be monitoring their progress in the beginning and could intervene if things were not going well. We knew that most of our recent high school graduates did not have the self-discipline to keep up with writing assignments (which most online courses require and which makes most online courses particularly difficult for students who are slow or poor writers), to keep up with posting thoughtful comments about their classmates' answers to questions (which most online courses require), or to take the initiative to communicate with a professor by email rather than in person when something was going wrong.

It is likely that most high school students do not have experience managing their own time when they are coming out of an institution where everything was scheduled for them. In fact, in "asynchronous" online courses (meaning that there are no scheduled class times where students and the professor are online together and that students access course sessions and assignments whenever it suits their schedule), we have seen some students forget about doing the classwork for a week or two since it does not appear on their class schedule; thus, they fall behind. For most college students who are coming right out of high school and are accustomed to the social environment of classmates who are interacting in a classroom together, online courses might feel a bit isolating. You can see that some of these concerns are much less serious for returning adult students, who come with more life experience—including in the real-world job market—and who have left their own high school experience far behind.

So, the benefits of online courses are obvious: virtually total flexibility in scheduling your "class" time and homework time (at least, with asynchronous courses), no time spent commuting to class, and the opportunity to study with a wide variety of colleges across the U.S. and abroad. Still, students (especially recent high school graduates) enrolling in online courses need to know what will be expected of them and need to think hard about whether they have the motivation and self-discipline needed to succeed.

[5]

College Study Abroad

THE PRACTICE OF SENDING college students to study abroad for at least part of their undergraduate degree coursework has exploded over the past several decades. Years ago, when far fewer U.S. college students in fewer majors went outside of the country to study, it was mostly students majoring in a foreign language or maybe anthropology or history or political science or art history. To many parents of that generation, foreign study was a classy, though unnecessary, ornament for a liberal arts degree.

Now that the world has seemingly gotten so much smaller, foreign study is a lot less frivolous. More colleges now make foreign study a regular part of college life. In fact, we have talked about colleges in our podcast where the vast majority of students study abroad and where students are required to study abroad. Take Centre College in Kentucky, for example, where about 85 percent of students study abroad at least once, and about 25 percent study abroad at least twice.

Furthermore, foreign study has become more valuable in a range of majors, including business, where study outside the U.S. can open up the world of international business to students, who can learn firsthand about our global economy before entering it. And, as always, studying a language in a non-English-speaking country where that language is spoken can open up a vast array of careers abroad, where near-fluency in that second language would be required.

Apart from the many practical reasons for studying abroad, the philosophical underpinning is that students who have been immersed in a different cultural setting, surrounded by people who are not exactly like them and who have political and religious beliefs that are not exactly like theirs, are likely to emerge as more flexible human beings, who are more open to diversity and who can more easily and more willingly examine issues from a variety of viewpoints as they go out into the world as adults.

Of course, study abroad is also super fun.

Part-Time Study Abroad

If a student is interested in exploring the culture of another country or working on some language skills, a short study abroad program could be the perfect opportunity. It could be for a summer or for a semester or even for a full school year.

If this is something that you know your teenager is interested in or if this is something you are interested in for your teenager, check out what study abroad options are available at colleges you are getting ready to put on your teenager's list. Colleges set up study abroad programs in various ways. A college might have its own study abroad program on its own campus in another country, or it might offer a program on the campus of a partner university in another country. Or a college might join a group of colleges that offer study abroad programs together in facilities in another country. Students typically go for one or both semesters during their junior year and take a full course load while there so they do not get behind in their progress toward graduation.

Or take a look at what the American Institute for Foreign Study (AIFS) has to offer. Based in Stamford, Connecticut, AIFS operates a wide range of summer, semester-long, and year-long programs in over 20 countries on five continents. Some summer programs are as short as three weeks—time enough to learn a lot, but not enough time to get homesick.

In AIFS programs, students take college courses taught in English and receive college credits, which can be transferred back to the student's own college. If a student chooses to attend a program in a non-English-speaking country, then language courses are usually required. For example, in just a one-semester program, which opens with an intensive full-time two-week language course before the semester starts and continues with regular language classes during the semester, students can earn a full year of foreign language credits, which many liberal arts students need to fulfill bachelor's degree requirements.

By the way, whatever financial aid students have at their home college can usually be used to cover the costs of attending a semester or two abroad, and AIFS has scholarships available for their programs as well. We have found that it can actually be cheaper to spend a semester abroad through AIFS than to pay for tuition and living expenses at a private college in the U.S. However, you should keep in mind that students usually cannot work while studying abroad because student visas have strict rules about that; so, money will have to come from somewhere else for daily expenses.

Clearly, there are things for parents to think about before sending a child off to Australia or South Africa or India or Brazil or China or Greece or Germany to study—even for three weeks in the summer, much less part time or full time during the academic year. One thing is safety, especially for countries that have had some recent political turmoil or history of discrimination. Another is medical insurance (typically provided through the program) and medical care in the event that your teenager becomes sick while abroad. For these reasons, going through an established program—whether one college's program or a group program like AIFS—is important. Established programs have a history of handling problems when they arise and typically have on-site residential and administrative staff to make sure your teenager is well supervised generally and well cared for in an emergency.

Another idea is to see whether colleges your teenager is interested in offer any kind of exchange program with other colleges. For example, New York University (NYU) offers one-semester exchange programs with three HBCUs (in the U.S.) as well as two universities in Puerto Rico. While Puerto Rico is a territory of the U.S., those universities do offer a kind of international experience in that the NYU exchange students would be immersed in a Spanish-speaking culture that is quite different from what they would be experiencing as NYU students in New York City.

Going to a Foreign College

So, what about a student who wants to go to a college that is located outside the U.S.? Of course, there are thousands of colleges available in many countries across the world—many of which have much longer and more remarkable histories than anything you can find here in the U.S. (but that's a different book). Admissions requirements, however, can be quite different from what U.S. colleges expect, partly because the systems of primary and secondary education in other countries are typically quite different from ours.

Full-time study abroad means even more "red tape" for families—including the complicated student visa application (which requires a relatively high minimum bank balance that will support the student) that must be completed and delivered to the U.S. consulates of foreign countries. (This is also true for many semester-long study abroad programs, though some U.S. colleges and AIFS help families handle that paperwork.) At foreign colleges outside English-speaking countries, classes will not be taught in English, so students need to make sure that their language skills can support academic study in that other language.

One unique choice for full-time study abroad is Richmond, the American International University in London. Richmond is accredited in both the U.S. and the United Kingdom so that admissions (there is a U.S. admissions office in Boston) and potential transfer of credits back to U.S. colleges are simplified. Richmond offers bachelor's and master's degree programs to students from over 100 countries. While it offers a lovely picture-postcard campus in Richmond for freshmen and sophomores and a location in the prestigious neighborhood of Kensington in London for juniors, seniors, and graduate students, Richmond also has two outstanding study abroad centers in Rome and Florence, Italy, where both the curricula and the settings are unbeatable. So both its locations and its students are truly international, but U.S. students have the comfort of taking classes in English. Incidentally, attending Richmond is no more expensive than attending a comparable private college in the U.S. (and tuition might actually be a little lower).

Here is a personal note about Richmond from Regina:

> *My middle child earned his bachelor's degree through full-time study at Richmond, and it was truly a priceless experience. Bobby graduated with an international network of friends and future colleagues and professors from dozens and dozens of countries. He and one of his classmates (a talented young woman from Turkey) founded The Workshop Collective, an international group of young artists and musicians who work together and perform together and support each other's endeavors. It all started with the international perspective that he got by studying in the U.K. None of that would have ever happened if Bobby had gone to college in the U.S. He was so happy at Richmond and in London that my daughter is headed there for graduate school, and he stayed on in London to get a master's degree from a British university.*

Another interesting choice is The American University of Paris (AUP), a small, but incredibly diverse, institution—as the brochure says, "1000 Students, 100 Nationalities." A liberal arts university founded in 1962, AUP is one of the oldest American higher education institutions in Europe. So, it's American, which might feel a lot more comfortable to American students than studying in a foreign university. It offers bachelor's degrees in a variety of arts and sciences, plus international business administration, and offers master's degrees in six fields. And did we say it's in Paris, possibly the most beautiful city in the world.

Other Ways To Study Abroad

One obvious choice is to have students wait until they are in graduate school to study abroad. Some U.S. colleges operate graduate programs abroad, and there are many graduate programs offered by foreign universities as well, of course. At that time in their lives, students will likely be more mature, will have a better handle on what they want to do for a career, will be more focused on making the best use of their time abroad, and might be able to assume more of the cost themselves.

Here is a personal note about graduate study abroad from Regina:

> *My oldest child chose to attend graduate school at the Valencia (Spain) campus of Berklee College of Music in Boston, where he had earned an undergraduate degree. It was Berklee's first year of offering graduate programs, and that made for a dynamic situation. Jimmy's graduate degree is in Global Entertainment and Music Business, and Europe was a great place to learn about international business and the international music industry. His friends in Valencia came from all over the world— many to get a graduate degree in music performance or film scoring— and now work all over the world. Study in Spain turned out to be an international career-making move for many of them.*

Another idea comes from some colleges (often faith-based colleges) that offer service trips abroad—sometimes for credit, sometimes not. Some trips might be as short as a week or two and might be run during college vacations. In addition to serving a good purpose and helping others, such trips are usually well supervised and carefully structured—all of which might make you feel better about sending your teenager on one.

[6]

What Are Your Deal Breakers?

Well, now that you have some background about the world of college, it's time to start making decisions about where your teenager should apply—tentative decisions anyway. In a minute, we are going to ask you to take out a pencil (literally or figuratively) and start checking off those tentative decisions, hopefully reached jointly with your teenager. But before you check off the first box, let's preview the "discussion guide" that follows.

A discussion guide is a road map that helps you navigate through important decisions. Like all road maps, it displays the options. A road map does not make the decisions. You have to do that. Now, all of the options, like all roads, have their particular attractions. Whenever you pick one, you might regret the roads not taken. But you do have to decide.

The discussion guide that follows provides reasonable options for decisions your family will have to make about the types of colleges your teenager should apply to and offers a few arguments in favor of each option. The arguments for each option are just about equivalent because each option is, in fact, the right choice for some families. You will have to discuss the options and choose the ones that are best for your family.

For some parents and for some teenagers, there is one criterion for choosing where to apply, and they are willing to consider any number of colleges of many different types that meet that one criterion. For example, the college has to be close to home. For other parents and for other teenagers, there are two—or more—criteria that have to be met. For example, the college has to be close to home and it has to be public.

As it turns out, some criteria are both very important to some families and not at all important to other families. You need to understand which criteria, if any, are critically important to you—your "deal breakers," we will call them. That understanding is a useful first step in narrowing down your teenager's college options among the more than 4,500 two-year and four-year degree-granting institutions in the U.S. (plus all of those outside the U.S.).

Let us also say that this is the right time for you to be honest with your teenager about what, if anything, is a deal breaker for you as a parent. For example, if you really cannot imagine letting your teenager go away to college, then college location is one of your deal breakers. You can then limit your teenager's choices to colleges close to home. Or if you really cannot imagine how you could pay for a private college (because no one can count on a full scholarship and you do not want to borrow tens of thousands of dollars from the federal government through a Direct PLUS loan for parents), then whether the college is public or private is one of your deal breakers. You can then narrow your teenager's choices down to public colleges. Ignoring your deal breakers now may cause some serious disappointment for your teenager later on. So have the conversation first. Think hard before you let your teenager fall in love with a college you have no intention of paying for him or her to attend. We have seen this happen way too many times.

Similarly, this is the time for your teenager to be honest with you about his or her own deal breakers. For example (and this is a true story), if your teenager is going to refuse to study hard in a science major (your idea) because her heart is set on studying music (her idea), then having the college major she wants available at a college becomes one of her deal breakers (just ask my young friend Camilla, who today is an accomplished film scorer and music professor, but who had a shaky start at a science and math college chosen for her by her parents). So, as we said, have the conversation.

Of course, there might not be any deal breakers for either you or your teenager, leaving your family the full range of colleges to consider. The sky is the limit. That makes life easier in some ways, but it means that you will have lots and lots of colleges to research.

So, let's begin our discussion guide of possible deal breakers. We are going to use the generic term "colleges" to include both colleges and universities, unless we occasionally want to make a particular point about universities.

If you'd like to download and print a summary version of the discussion guide, just sign up for our email list: http://policystudies.org/subscribe.

1. Colleges Away from Home or Close to Home?

For many students in the U.S. over a couple of centuries now, going away to college has been a rite of passage. Trunks are packed, car trips are taken, and teary good-byes are said in a dorm room on a campus of ivy-covered buildings. Hundreds of movies and televisions shows picture college kids doing crazy things on those campuses in those dorms or in fraternity and sorority houses. In some ways, the idea of kids going away to college has been part of the American dream.

Sometimes it is the parent who thinks the teenager should go away and have a new experience and the teenager who wants to stay home, though you might think it would usually be the reverse. Either way, is college location a deal breaker in putting colleges on your teenager's list—that is, will you put only colleges away from home on your list or only colleges close to home on your list? Is college location a deal breaker for you?

❏ **Only colleges away from home.** That is not just a notion from the idealized past. Today, there are still many reasons why students want to go away to college and indeed why students should go away to college. By the way, you are going to have to define "away from home" in conversation with your teenager. Do you mean colleges in another region of the country, or colleges in another state (even if it is the state next door to yours), or colleges in another part of your home state (if your state is large enough)? Do you include colleges outside the U.S. that are really far away? Let's look at four reasons for students to go away to college:

- It is a chance to grow up. Clearly, many 17- and 18-year-olds like the idea of living away from the daily oversight of their families. Who can blame them? This is their first step in making their own unsupervised decisions about academic issues and about social interactions—about what courses to take, when to schedule their classes, what to do on weekends and with whom, how to manage their time and their money, and more. Going away to college is their first step at separating from their families and becoming the adults they are soon to be. Everyone has to do it. Is there a better way to learn how to live on your own or a better time to learn it?

- It is a chance to live in a different geographical location. If a student grew up in the city, it is a chance to live in the country or in the suburbs. If a student grew up in the Northeast, it is a chance to see the South or the West or the Midwest. If a student grew up in the U.S., it is a chance to experience life in Europe or in Asia or in Africa or in South America. You get the idea. There is a lot to be said for going to college outside of your hometown or home state or home region or home country. Is there a better way to learn what other places are like or a better time to learn it?

- It is a chance to live in a different social setting with people who are not like you. If a student did not grow up and attend school in a multiethnic, multicultural, and racially diverse setting, going away to college is a way to broaden that student's personal experiences with lots of people of different backgrounds. Learning how to work with people of all backgrounds is a life skill most students will need in their futures. Is there a

67

better way to learn what other people are like or a better time to learn it?

- It is a chance to attend a college with a special focus or to major in a particular field a student cannot get close to home. If a student wants to attend a single-sex college or a faith-based college or a military service academy or an HBCU, for example, that student might have to leave home to find it. If a student has an interest in a college that focuses solely on one academic field (for example, fine arts), that student might have to leave home to find it. If a student has a strong interest in a certain academic field (for example, computer science or journalism or linguistics or civil engineering or theater or mathematics), that student might have to leave home to find a college that has a well-regarded major in that field. Of course, students might change their minds once they get there, but these are still reasons to look at colleges away from home.

❏ **Only colleges close to home.** There are at least as many reasons for students to stay close to home for college—sometimes living at home and sometimes living on campus or in a nearby apartment. By the way, you are going to have to define "close to home" in conversation with your teenager. Do you mean only colleges in your hometown? Do you include colleges in your region of your home state? Do you include colleges anywhere in your home state? Of course, colleges anywhere in your home state if your home state is Rhode Island is not the same as colleges anywhere in your home state if your home state is Texas. Let's look at four reasons for students to stay close to home for college:

- It is a way to save money. This is a complicated reason,

because it is possible that a student will get an amazing scholarship, which also covers living costs, at a college far from home. In that case, it is possible that going away actually saves the family money. However, it is fair to say that most students do not get full scholarships, including living expenses; so, for most students, going to college in or near their hometown saves money. Staying close to home for college saves even more money if the college is a public college, where tuition will be far lower for residents than tuition would be at a private college anywhere or even at a public college in another state. And staying close to home for college saves still more money if the student actually lives at home and attends a public college. But, remember that it is complicated. For example, going away to a public college in a different part of your home state is likely cheaper than staying in your hometown and attending a private college, even if the student lives at home.

- It is a way to keep a student involved in the family culture. For some families, cultural traditions in the family or in the community are very important, like attending the family's church and participating in church activities or being part of social groups that represent the family's ethnic or cultural background. For these families, sending a child away to college breaks the social and familial bonds that are very much a part of that family's lifestyle. Whether the family could adjust to that sort of break—or would want to—would need to be the topic of a serious discussion.

- It is a way to give a student a little more time to get ready to be on his or her own. Some 17- and 18-year-olds are not quite ready to live on their own too far from home. That is especially true of young people who have not traveled very much with their families, who have not attended camps or summer study programs away from home, who have not participated in very many outside-of-school activities, or who are younger than the typical high school graduate (including some bright students who graduate early). For such students, a nearby college might allow for a more comfortable, less anxious transition for both the parent and the student.

- It is a way for a student to attend a great college that happens to be in the student's hometown. As a matter of fact, sometimes a great college—or even the perfect college—for a student happens to be located in or near the student's hometown. For example, it has the right academic program or the right special focus, it is highly respected, and the student has good enough high school grades and college admission test scores to get in. When that is the case, going away to college just to go away does not really make sense. (Regina learned this from her daughter, a dancer who was accepted at the prestigious Ailey/Fordham B.F.A. Program in Dance, located right in their hometown of New York City. Though she was accepted at other excellent dance programs as well, her daughter said, "Why would I leave New York City to major in dance when most dancers in the country are trying their hardest to come to New York City to dance?" She had a point. She stayed, lived on campus at Lincoln Center to get a little of that "being away" feeling, and graduated in May, 2015. She loved every minute.)

❏ **It doesn't matter—colleges away from home and/or close to home.** In other words, college location is not a deal breaker for you. You are willing to have your teenager go away to college, and you are just about as willing to have him or her stay close to home for college. College choice for you is not about location. So, colleges near and far might show up on your teenager's list. Presumably, your teenager agrees.

2. Two-Year or Four-Year Colleges?

In Chapter 2, we talked a lot about two-year colleges *vs.* four-year colleges and the pros and cons of each. Now consider whether the number of years of study and type of degree a college offers is a deal breaker in putting colleges on your teenager's list—that is, will you put *only two-year* colleges on your teenager's list or *only four-year* colleges on your teenager's list?

❏ **Only two-year colleges.** Remember that when we are talking about two-year colleges, we are talking mostly about public community colleges, which typically award associate's degrees. Let's look at the reasons in favor of them:
- Two-year colleges offer their students core liberal arts courses (which can often be transferred to four-year colleges later) and/or technical training in many different fields at a very low price. Putting only two-year colleges on your list now is a reasonable decision if paying for college—either right away for a two-year degree or eventually for a four-year degree—is a critical concern for your family.
- Two-year colleges offer associate's degrees, which can be enough for some careers, including high-paying technical careers. Later, if the student wants to do

so, the credits earned for an associate's degree can be transferred to four-year colleges and applied toward credits needed for a four-year bachelor's degree. (In fact, some two-year colleges in some states are now authorized to offer bachelor's degrees, especially in technical fields where workers in the labor force are in short supply. Students pursuing those bachelor's degrees would need to stay at the two-year college longer, of course.)

- Two-year colleges offer students who have struggled in high school a chance to improve their academic record and gain the fundamental skills and study habits they will need to succeed in more advanced college study. After doing well at a two-year college, such students can get into a better four-year college than they could have gotten into right out of high school.

- Two-year colleges can be a good choice if a student is undecided about an academic field of study in college and/or about a future career. Trying out different academic majors and different programs leading to different career paths is cheaper and likely easier to do at a two-year college than at a four-year college.

❑ **Only four-year colleges.** Four-year colleges come in all shapes and sizes, and there is probably one that would be a good fit for almost any student. The range of four-year colleges is so broad in what they offer, where they are located, how much they cost, and how selective they are that choosing to put only four-year colleges on your teenager's list still leaves a lot of options open. Let's look at the reasons in favor of four-year institutions:

- If you and your teenager believe that a bachelor's degree is what your teenager wants to earn and if he or she is ready to tackle the academic work at a four-year college, then getting on that track right out of high school could be the smoothest and most efficient course to take. Some research studies suggest that students do better in the long run in terms of the highest degree earned when they attend the most selective college that will admit them at the beginning, which would be a four-year college rather than a two-year college.

- There is, admittedly, some prestige that goes along with attending a four-year college rather than a two-year college, partly because they are more selective in admitting students.

- A four-year college is more likely to have a traditional college atmosphere (e.g., dormitory living, big varsity sports, fraternities and sororities) and is more likely to have younger students than two-year colleges, which have a larger proportion of returning adult students.

- Starting at a four-year college saves having to go through the application process all over again at the end of a two-year program. As it turns out, lots of two-year college graduates do not end up going on to four-year colleges, for whatever reasons.

❑ **It doesn't matter—two-year and/or four-year colleges.** In other words, the number of years of study and type of degree offered is not a deal breaker for you. You are willing to have your teenager go to a two-year college and earn an associate's degree, at least as the first step, and you are also willing to have him or her go straight to a four-year college in pursuit of a bachelor's degree. College choice for you is not about whether it is a two-year or four-year institution. So, both types of institutions might show up on your teenager's list. Presumably, your teenager agrees.

3. Public or Private Colleges?

In Chapter 1, we talked a lot about public *vs.* private *vs.* proprietary institutions and the pros and cons of each. The question now is whether your family wants to consider both public institutions and private institutions (by the way, all proprietary schools are private) for your teenager's first step into higher education. Is the likely cost of a college education a deal breaker in putting colleges on your teenager's list—that is, will you put *only public* colleges on your teenager's list or *only private* colleges on your teenager's list?

❑ **Only public colleges.** Remember that when we are talking about public institutions, we are talking about public two-year community colleges as well as public four-year colleges. Let's look at the reasons in favor of them:

- The main factor here, of course, is cost. Public colleges are less expensive than private colleges when it comes to tuition, and public two-year community colleges are even less expensive than public four-year colleges. However, considering the cost of college can be complicated, as we have said. A private college that offers your teenager a substantial scholarship could turn out to cost your family less than a public college that does not offer you any scholarship money. But, you cannot count on a scholarship; and, even if your teenager gets a good scholarship, it might still leave tens of thousands of dollars not covered by the scholarship. And working while in school to make up even part of the difference is very, very demanding for most students.

- For many students, the public flagship state university is the place to be. Just remember, the best and the brightest high school students who live in the state really want to go to their flagship state university. Why? Because these universities are relatively inexpensive, academically respectable, well regarded across the state and across the country, often very competitive in sports arenas, chocked full of student clubs and activities, within driving distance of home, and a social hub for lots of their high school classmates. What could be better?

- Public colleges tend to be larger than private colleges. If your teenager likes the idea of a big school with lots of students and professors and student clubs and varsity sports, then a public college will provide all that— at a lower cost than a private college.

- Many public colleges have more prestige than many private colleges. There is certainly no reason to pay more to go to a private college that is not as highly respected nationally as a great public college.

☐ **Only private colleges.** Remember that when we are talking about private institutions, we are talking about everything from very small liberal arts colleges to quite large universities. Let's look at the reasons in favor of them:

- Private colleges would seem to cost more than public colleges. However, as we have said, figuring the cost of college can be complicated. A private college that offers your teenager a "full ride"—that is, a scholarship that covers tuition and housing—could turn out to cost your family less than a public college that does not offer you any scholarship money.

- There is undeniably a prestige factor, particularly in some parts of the country, in attending private colleges, at least the best ones.

- Institutions with a special academic focus—especially in the arts (music, dance, visual arts)—and institutions abroad tend to be private. If your teenager is interested in one of those, private institutions are the way to go.

- For good students who are not sure what they want to study in college or what they want to do after college, a small private liberal arts college offering a well-rounded education could be the best steppingstone for the future.

❏ **It doesn't matter—public and/or private colleges.** In other words, if the best choice for your teenager could be a public college or could be a private college—because of majors being offered or location or size or special focus or even family sentiment—then public *vs.* private college is not a deal breaker for you. You are willing to have your teenager go to either. So, both types of colleges might show up on your teenager's list. Presumably, your teenager agrees.

4. Large or Small Colleges?

The question here is whether your family wants to consider both large and small colleges. You will need to consider both the academic and social environment for your teenager. Is the size of the student body a deal breaker in putting colleges on your list— that is, will you put *only large* colleges on your teenager's list or *only small* colleges on your teenager's list?

❏ **Only large colleges.** Remember that when we are talking about large institutions, we are talking about both two-year and four-year colleges and about both public and private colleges. Let's look at the reasons in favor of large colleges:

- Large colleges with more students and, therefore, more professors likely offer more courses and a greater variety of majors to choose from. Many large universities have an impressive number of schools/colleges within them (sometimes a dozen or more) and an impressive number of majors to choose from (sometimes 100 or more). Typically, they offer more to choose from academically than small institutions.

- Large colleges have more laboratories and libraries and theaters and sports facilities, which are needed to serve a larger student body.

- Large colleges have more student organizations and clubs on campus to meet every possible interest a student has—sometimes hundreds and hundreds.

- Large colleges have more social activities available, including more fraternities and sororities.

- Large colleges likely have more varsity men's and women's sports teams of a higher caliber, and attending major sports events is more likely part of college life.

- There are more alumni to help connect students to the real world after graduation.

❏ **Only small colleges.** Remember that when we are talking about small institutions, we are most likely talking about private four-year colleges (though we could be talking about a small branch campus of a large public two-year community college or four-year university that is located in a different town from the main campus). Let's look at the reasons in favor of small colleges:

- Great small liberal arts colleges might provide smart students with the most challenging college education available. Students at these colleges will likely be engaged regularly in classroom discussions with professors and with their peers and will more likely have a chance to do research projects with professors.

- Small colleges have more small classes, thus affording students more attention from professors and making it more likely that full professors will be teaching the courses (rather than graduate teaching assistants). You can tell that small classes are important because most large colleges actually advertise the number of small classes they are able to offer.

- A student is less likely to "get lost" at a small college, where more professors and administrators (like deans) and counselors are likely to know a student's name and background. For a student who is worried about making the transition to college (or for the parent of such a student), having more personal relationships with college personnel can make the difference between success and failure.

- Small colleges are probably more nurturing than large colleges, because a variety of staff members can be more encouraging of and involved with students who are struggling.

- It is easier to join student clubs and play on sports teams when there are not quite so many other students trying to do the same thing.

- Some people believe that it is better to be a big fish in a little pond—that is, a student is more likely to be able to make a name for himself or herself at a small college.

❑ **It doesn't matter—large and/or small colleges.** In other words, the size of the student body is not a deal breaker for you. You are willing to have your teenager go to a large college, a small college, or a medium-sized college in between. So, knowing that there are advantages and disadvantages to each, colleges of all sizes—from student bodies of under 1,000 to over 35,000 might show up on your teenager's list. Presumably, your teenager agrees.

5. Urban, Suburban, or Rural Colleges?

While the type of community the college is located in might not seem nearly so important as the academic and financial issues we have already discussed, it is a lot more important than you might think for some students and some families. Some students are dying to get away from the type of community they grew up in, and others cannot imagine fitting in or being comfortable in a new physical and social environment. Obviously, there are advantages and disadvantages to urban, suburban, and rural settings, most of which are common sense. Is the college's community setting a deal breaker in putting colleges on your teenager's list—that is, will you put *only urban* colleges on your teenager's list, *only suburban* colleges on your teenager's list, or *only rural* colleges on your teenager's list? This time, you might want to consider checking off *two* options— like suburban and rural, if you can imagine sending your teenager to suburban or rural campuses, but not to an urban campus, for example.

❑ **Only urban colleges.** Remember that when we are talking about urban institutions, we are talking about all types of colleges that are located in cities, including some very small colleges that are located in some very big cities. Let's look at the reasons in favor of urban colleges:

- Many students and parents like urban campuses because of the general excitement that cities offer and the many cultural opportunities that are available (e.g., museums, theaters, concert halls, public libraries, places to take music and dance lessons).

- Cities usually have substantial ethnic, racial, and cultural diversity among their residents, which can make people from all kinds of backgrounds feel comfortable. Urban colleges likely have a similar kind of diversity among their college students, making for interesting and thoughtful social and intellectual interactions among the students.

- Living in a dormitory at an urban college is a relatively safe and protected way to enjoy life in a big city for several years as a young adult.

- Urban campuses usually offer students easy access to city sights and neighborhoods by public transportation (in some cities more than in others). Students who grew up in cities and did not drive cars as teenagers find this access to public transportation especially helpful. Students at suburban and rural colleges are much more likely to need a car at some point, thus raising the cost of attending those colleges.

- Most cities have a variety of colleges within their boundaries, giving students the opportunity to meet a variety of college students and share their interests in groups outside of their own campus.

❑ **Only suburban colleges.** Remember that when we are

talking about suburban institutions, we are talking about all types of colleges that are located in suburban areas close to, but outside of cities. Let's look at the reasons in favor of suburban colleges:

- Suburban campuses have fewer safety issues—or, at least, fewer perceived safety issues—than urban campuses, making them a more comfortable choice for some students and some parents.
- Suburban campuses likely have fewer off-campus distractions from studying compared to urban campuses.
- It is likely cheaper to live in the suburbs than in cities—even if students are living on campus—when you take into account the costs of movies, drug store items, occasional or regular off-campus meals, and the like.
- Suburban colleges might have the ideal location because they are close enough to a city to enjoy what cities have to offer, without being in the middle of one, and are not as remote as rural colleges, where there is relatively little going on off campus.

❏ **Only rural colleges.** Remember that when we are talking about rural institutions, we are talking about all types of colleges that are located in rural areas in what most people would think of as "the country." Let's look at the reasons in favor of rural colleges:

- Rural campuses likely have fewer safety issues on and off the campus compared to colleges in other types of communities.
- There are even fewer distractions from studying in the evenings and on weekends.
- It is likely cheapest to live in rural college communities, whether living on or off campus.

- Many students appreciate the unspoiled environment of a rural campus—great for outdoor sports, like hiking or biking.
- For some students and some parents, a rural campus is the idyllic college campus—that is, one where students are disconnected from the everyday trials and tribulations that would be part of daily life in cities and even in suburbs.

❏ **It doesn't matter—urban, suburban, and/or rural colleges.** In other words, the type of community a college is located in is not a deal breaker for you. You are willing to have your teenager go to an urban, suburban, or rural college. So, colleges in all types of community settings might show up on your teenager's list. Presumably, your teenager agrees.

6. Colleges with Certain Majors?

As we discussed in Chapter 4, some colleges are known for their academic specialties, like music or art or engineering or business. Some specialized colleges teach only that subject—like Berklee College of Music. Others have strong specialized schools or colleges within a larger university—like the School of Hotel Administration at Cornell University. Others have strong departments in certain fields—like the modern language departments at Middlebury College.

Some students have a particular college major in mind when they are just juniors or seniors in high school. Some majors are easy to find and are offered by most (though not all) colleges—like English and mathematics and history. Other majors are harder to find because every college doesn't offer them—especially technical majors, like architecture and engineering and computer science.

Of course, many students will change their minds about a major after a month or a year or even two years in college. So, is the availability of a certain major a deal breaker in putting colleges on your teenager's list—that is, will you put *only* colleges with certain majors on your teenager's list?

❏ **Only colleges with certain majors.** Remember that these colleges could be public or private, large or small, and located just about anywhere. Let's look at the reasons in favor of colleges with certain majors:

- A student who has thought hard about a field of study to pursue in college should use that as a way to narrow down his or her choice of colleges. There is no point in researching and applying to small liberal arts colleges if the student really wants to major in engineering.
- A student who has thought hard about a field of study to pursue in college should be looking at the best programs in the country in that major—if he or she has the high school grades and college admission test scores to get into the colleges with the best programs.
- Families of such students should discuss how likely it is that the student will continue down that path in order to decide how specialized the colleges on the list should be. For example, a student interested in a music major might want to leave some options open by not applying only to music conservatories, but also to universities that offer a music major along with many other majors.

❏ **It doesn't matter—colleges with or without certain majors.** In other words, the existence of certain majors is not a deal breaker for you—perhaps because your teenager has not voiced an interest in a certain major, perhaps because you don't agree with the major your teenager is interested in, perhaps because you believe that your teenager would change his or her mind about the major if your teenager were accepted by the right college, perhaps because you believe that college students switch majors all the time anyway. To you, finding the best college is more important than whether it has any certain major. Presumably, your teenager agrees.

7. Colleges with Certain Activities?

Sometimes an extracurricular activity is just as important to a teenager—and even to a parent—as the academics at a college. Sports teams are probably the prime example. Your family might be looking for—rather, insisting on—a college with a competitive football, swimming, track, basketball, lacrosse, or crew program and so on. Sports teams could be a deal breaker for both young men and young women, of course.

We would like to imagine that other activities would have the same appeal or attraction as sports—for example, a great school newspaper, glee club, drama group, or community service organization.

One more thing to say about sports: If your teenager has not been playing on high-powered high school teams or competitive community teams and has not been in serious talks with college recruiters before you start making your college list, he or she is not going to get a big sports scholarship. Some high school seniors, who have not talked to any college recruiters or coaches, still harbor the dream that a sports scholarship is the way they will get to college and that professional sports is the way they will make a living after that. That could not be less likely.

So, is the availability of a certain activity a deal breaker in putting colleges on your teenager's list—that is, will you put *only* colleges with certain activities on your teenager's list?

❑ **Only colleges with certain activities.** Remember that these colleges could be public or private, large or small, and located just about anywhere. Let's look at the reasons in favor of colleges with certain activities:

- A student who is passionate about a certain activity and who has done a lot with that activity while in high school might indeed want to continue with it in college—whether it is journalistic or artistic or athletic or service oriented or something else. It is important for students in college to have some activities that help them make a fuller life for themselves outside of the academics in the classroom. Having activities to enjoy, to sharpen teamwork skills in, to develop leadership skills in, and to make close friends from is a big part of college life.

- A student who is really talented and accomplished in something outside of the classroom—like drama or sports—should be looking for colleges that have respected activities in those fields. Getting to use those talents and skills—and perhaps being recognized for them—can be important in keeping a student happy in college and even later in life.

- Families of such students should discuss how likely it is that the student will continue to participate in that certain activity once in college. For example, a student who is the editor of the high school newspaper might not really have the interest to pursue newspaper writing in college, which can be a daily affair rather than once a week or once a month like in high school. Or a student who wrestled in high school might not want to give up the amount of time—study time and social time—it would take to wrestle on a competitive team in college. But it takes a parent or an adult with some experience in life to talk with a student about how they could benefit from keeping up with activities in college. Yes, it might be harder logistically or more time consuming, but it can certainly pay off.

❏ **It doesn't matter—colleges with or without certain activities.** In other words, the existence of certain activities is not a deal breaker for you—perhaps because your teenager has not voiced enough of an interest in a certain activity, perhaps because you don't care whether your teenager pursues that interest, perhaps because you believe that your teenager would change his or her mind about the importance of that activity if he or she were accepted by the right college, perhaps because you believe that college students start and drop activities all the time. To you, finding the best college is more important than whether it has any certain activity or sports team. Presumably, your teenager agrees.

8. Colleges with a Specific Mission?

Some colleges have a specific mission that drives their students' academic and social lives. Some colleges are known for the student population they were founded to serve, others by the special academic programs they offer, others for the philosophy that underpins the institution. Is a college's specific mission a deal breaker in putting colleges on your teenager's list—that is, will you put *only* colleges with a specific mission on your teenager's list? Here are a number to choose from (you might even check *more than one* because they are not necessarily mutually exclusive—for example, there are faith-based HBCUs and there are single-sex HBCUs and there are single-sex faith-based colleges).

❑ **Only faith-based colleges.** Remember that when we are talking about faith-based colleges, we are talking about private colleges, which might be large or small and which might be located in urban, suburban, or rural settings. They might be of any faith. Let's look at the reasons in favor of faith-based colleges:

- Families that have a strong religious affiliation and take part in religious observances and activities outside of regular worship services would probably find the atmosphere and sense of community at faith-based colleges established by their own religion to their liking.

- Students who went to faith-based high schools are likely to feel at home in faith-based colleges, both with the faculty and with other students.

- Parents who are worried about allowing their teenager to go to a college far from home or in an urban setting might feel more comfortable if that college were a faith-based institution, which likely provides students with more support and supervision.

- Some parents and students—regardless of their own religion—are drawn to the emphasis on service to others that characterizes many faith-based colleges.

- Many parents and students—regardless of their own religion—are drawn to the excellent long-standing academic reputations of the nation's top faith-based colleges.

☐ **Only single-sex colleges.** Remember that when we are talking about single-sex colleges, we are talking about a small number of private colleges, which tend to be smaller colleges and which might be located in urban, suburban, or rural settings. There are just a handful of all-men's colleges and just over 40 all-women's colleges. Some are quite well known, but many are not. Let's look at the reasons in favor of single-sex colleges:

- Some educators and most alumni/alumnae of single-sex colleges believe that students pay more attention to their studies and, thus, are likely to do better academically when they attend single-sex colleges and are likely do better in graduate study and in their careers thereafter.
- Some educators and most alumni/alumnae of single-sex colleges believe that students have more opportunities in class and outside of class in campus organizations to develop their own leadership skills when they attend single-sex colleges.
- Students who went to single-sex high schools and enjoyed their high school experience are likely to feel at home in single-sex colleges.
- Parents of girls who are worried about allowing their daughters to go to a college far from home or in an urban setting might feel more comfortable if that college were a single-sex institution that helped develop confidence and a strong sense of self in their students.
- Some parents and students are drawn to the histories and traditions of well-known single-sex colleges and

are impressed by their famous alumni/alumnae.

- Many parents and students are drawn to the excellent long-standing academic reputations of the nation's top single-sex colleges.

❑ **Only HBCUs.** Remember that when we are talking about historically black colleges and universities, we are talking about both public and private colleges, which might be small or medium-sized and which might be located in urban, suburban, or rural settings. They do not serve only black students, though the majority (and sometimes the vast majority) of their students are likely to be black. Some HBCUs are single-sex colleges, but more are faith-based colleges. Some are quite well known, but many are not. Let's look at the reasons in favor of HBCUs:

- Some educators and most alumni/alumnae of HBCUs believe that black students do better academically when they attend HBCUs—in part because more personal and academic support is likely available to them, especially to students who are the first in their families to attend college.
- Some educators and most alumni/alumnae of HBCUs believe that students have more opportunities in class and outside of class in campus organizations to develop their own leadership skills when they attend HBCUs.
- Students who went to high schools with a majority of black students are likely to feel at home at HBCUs.
- Some black parents and students are drawn to the remarkable histories and traditions of many of the older HBCUs (especially the ones established just before or after the Civil War) and are impressed by their illustri-

ous alumni/alumnae.

- Many black parents and students are drawn to the excellent academic reputations of the nation's top HBCUs.

❏ **It doesn't matter—faith-based colleges, single-sex colleges, and/or HBCUs.** In other words, none of these types of colleges with specific missions is interesting enough to you to make it a deal breaker. You are willing to have your teenager consider any or none of these, and some might show up on your teenager's list. Presumably, your teenager agrees.

❏ **No faith-based colleges, single-sex colleges, and/or HBCUs.** Alternatively, you might *not* be willing to consider some of these types of colleges for your teenager, and those would certainly *not* show up on your teenager's list. Which of these would you *eliminate* from consideration?
  ❏ **No faith-based colleges**
  ❏ **No single-sex colleges**
  ❏ **No HBCUs**

9. Colleges with a Special Relationship to the Student's Family or High School?

This can be a surprisingly influential factor for students and for their families in making a college decision. Is a college's relationship to your family or to your teenager's high school a deal breaker in putting colleges on your teenager's list—that is, will you put *only* colleges with such a relationship on your teenager's list? Here are the choices (you might even check *both* because they are not necessarily mutually exclusive—for example, there might be a college that has a relationship both with your family and with your teenager's high school).

❏ **Only colleges with a relationship to your family.** Remember that this category potentially includes colleges of all types. Let's look at the reasons in favor of these colleges:

- If either parent works at a college and, even better, gets free or reduced tuition for any children who enroll, this is a tough relationship to discount, especially if money is an issue. Even putting money aside, parents likely feel comfortable with and/or proud of the college they work for, and students themselves might feel comfortable going there because they are already familiar with it.

- Many students attend—or want to attend—the alma mater of their parents or grandparents. We see even first-generation college students (whose parents did not attend college) strongly considering the college attended by an older sibling. Family college connections can mean a lot—just like any other family traditions. This is especially true if students grew up with family members telling stories about their great times at college or telling students how truly excellent their college was and continues to be.

- Having family members or close friends living where a college is located can actually give a family a sense of a personal connection. Families might have heard about college events attended on the campus—sports events or concerts or lectures or service days or something else. Families might have seen the campus and thought about how attractive it was. Certainly, a parent who is reluctant to send a child to a college far away from home might be less anxious if a family member or close friend lived there—just in case of an emergency. For a student, too, having some family members or family friends nearby might ease the homesickness that comes with most students' first days on campus.

❑ **Only colleges with a relationship to your teenager's high school.** Remember that this category potentially includes colleges of all types. Let's look at the reasons in favor of these colleges:

- Some high schools have a relationship already built with a college, usually a nearby college. A noteworthy example of this is the growing number of Early College high schools, which have a carefully worked out agreement with a partner college, typically to provide college credit courses to students while they are still in high school and frequently to admit those students into the college almost automatically, thus allowing a seamless transition from high school to college. It is hard to make a case for giving up the advantages of this already-in-place relationship.

- Some high schools have arrangements with one or more colleges whereby students can take college courses for credit while in high school, banking those credits to transfer later to whatever college they attend; of course, it is even easier for those students to continue at the college where they have already earned those credits. Any of these arrangements between high schools and colleges can give students a streamlined pathway into a college, thus saving the time and effort and money expended in the typical application process. If your high school has such an arrangement with a college and if your teenager has taken advantage of it, it would be very hard to walk away from choosing that college as your only option—even if just for the first year or two.

❑ **It doesn't matter—colleges with or without a special relationship to the family or high school.** In other words, it is not a deal breaker if a college does or does not have a special relationship to your family or your teenager's high school. (Admittedly, having either of these relationships as a deal breaker would radically limit the number of colleges on your teenager's list. Of course, that could make it very easy for you, if you know your teenager can be admitted to that college and be happy there.) You are willing to have your teenager consider any of these—or none of these—and some might show up on your teenager's list. Presumably, your teenager agrees.

[7]

Just a Few More Questions Before Making Your List of Colleges

SO, YOUR DEAL BREAKERS are tentatively set. It is almost time to choose the colleges that are in keeping with those deal breakers. For example, you might be looking for large public four-year colleges close to home in an urban setting. Or just the opposite. Or faith-based colleges with business majors and great varsity sports teams. Or whatever you said when you were checking off boxes in Chapter 6.

Unless you were unusually limiting in what you decided, there will probably be many colleges still in contention when you apply your deal breakers to the thousands of colleges available to you in the U.S. (plus those abroad)—many more than your teenager can actually apply to. So, here are a few more questions to think about.

1. Selective or Not So Selective Colleges?

This question is the one most high school guidance counselors bring up first. You have probably heard people say that a student should apply to a "safety" school that he or she is sure to be admitted to; a couple of "reach" schools that would be great, but might be beyond or just beyond what the student's high school record warrants; and then some others in the middle that the student has a reasonable chance of being admitted to, though not guaranteed. That is really common sense.

As for a safety school, consider public community colleges and public four-year colleges (especially branch campuses of your state flagship public university, rather than the main campus, or a second-tier state system of public colleges that is not as prestigious as the state flagship university system). Some states have more public options than others, thus providing an array of safety school choices.

A real question comes in deciding whether to add to your teenager's list private four-year colleges that would serve as safety schools. It is our opinion that private colleges that could reasonably serve as safety schools for most high school students are not likely to be better than well-regarded public colleges available in a student's home state. If your teenager would not really want to go to that private safety school, why put it on the list? Why would you waste time applying? Why would you pay more money to go to a college that is not better? That's something to think hard about.

As for "reach" schools, keep in mind that applying to colleges is time consuming and expensive (unless you have application-fee waivers from the colleges, which are sometimes based on family income and sometimes based on a student's excellent high school record). Applying to reach schools that are significantly more selective than a student's high school grades and SAT or ACT scores would warrant might just be a waste of time. Should your teenager rule out applying to the most selective schools, given the chances that being admitted are slim, even if he or she is a good student? Perhaps consider applying to two or three—but only if your teenager is truly interested in going there.

Let's pause for a moment while considering how selective the colleges on your teenager's list should be. As you might realize yourself, every student's high school record is not as perfect as his or her parents might wish. The two most common problems are that the GPA (that is, the grade point average of high school courses) is not as high as it could be or should be *or* that the SAT and/or ACT scores (that is, the scores on the standardized college admission tests) are not as high as they could be or should be. Either of these problems makes choosing to put truly selective colleges on your teenager's list a risky move.

Who is in the more difficult situation? Is it a student whose high school GPA is lower than ideal for whatever reason—sports teams, time-consuming hobbies or other outside activities, interest in the opposite sex, laziness, mediocre teachers, or family issues? Or is it a student whose SAT and/or ACT scores are lower than ideal for whatever reason—unfamiliarity with the test, refusal to study for the test or to take practice tests, unavailability or unaffordability of a prep course to get ready for the test, test anxiety, or just a lackadaisical attitude toward standardized tests or college preparation generally? Let's look at these two cases.

STUDENTS WITH MEDIOCRE OR LOW SAT/ACT SCORES. What do we mean by mediocre or low scores? Let's take the SAT as the example.

If a student scores below 600 on any SAT subtest, that is a mediocre or low score. Scores in the low 600s are going to be problematic for most selective colleges, too.

However, having mediocre or low test scores is likely an easier problem to solve than having mediocre or low high school grades. While students' test scores are important to most top-ranked colleges, there are some colleges—including some really good colleges—that do not put so high a priority, or indeed any priority at all, on these test scores.

If you read the admissions blurbs on college websites, you will quickly see quite a few colleges that declare that SAT and/or ACT scores are not as important as high school grades and that the real picture of a student comes from the long and hard work the student has—or has not—done in courses (preferably rigorous courses) during the high school years. Those colleges will state that high school grades will tell them more about a student—about the student's determination and perseverance and motivation, for example—than his or her performance on one test given on one Saturday morning. Indeed, they will cite research that says that high school grades are a better predictor of college success than standardized test scores—for all of the reasons that common sense would tell you.

For years, a relatively small number of colleges had said that SAT and/or ACT scores were not required in their admissions process. More recently, more colleges have been added to this list—so many, in fact, that this group of colleges now has a name: "test-optional" colleges. One relatively recent addition to that list is prestigious Bryn Mawr College. Professor Marc Schulz, a member of the Bryn Mawr admissions committee was quoted on the Bryn Mawr

College website in July, 2014, as saying this: "We looked not just at the national data, but also took a very hard look at our own data over the last several years. It was clear that the standardized tests added very little predictive information after accounting for the strength of applicants' academic work in high school and the admissions staff's review of the whole application."

As of this writing (and colleges get added to this group every year), here are a few more highly respected colleges that do not require SAT or ACT scores for admission, although a student may usually submit the scores if he or she feels they will help the application: American University, Bard College, Bates College, Bennington College, Bowdoin College, Brandeis University, Hampshire College, Mount Holyoke College, Sarah Lawrence College, Smith College, Wake Forest University, and Wesleyan University.

Now, there are also "test-flexible" colleges. These are colleges that give students a choice of which standardized test scores to submit during the application process. Some of these policies are more "flexible" than others. Here are a few highly respected colleges that give students some flexibility in choosing which test scores to submit: Colby College, Colorado College, Hamilton College, Middlebury College, and New York University.

By the way, you can search for and find all kinds of lists of "test-optional" and "test-flexible" colleges online. However, because admissions policies change from time to time, you really need to check on a college's website to tell just exactly how the college does or does not require or use SAT or ACT scores. For example, some colleges require standardized test scores for some applicants, like homeschooled students and international students, but not for others, like students who are U.S. citizens and went to high school in the U.S.

You can find a list of "test-optional" and "test-flexible" colleges on the National Center for Fair and Open Testing website.

STUDENTS WITH MEDIOCRE OR LOW HIGH SCHOOL GRADES. What do we mean by mediocre or low high school grades? If a student has a GPA below 3.0, that is a mediocre or low GPA. GPAs of 3.0 to 3.3 are going to be problematic for most selective colleges, too. If the high school GPA is on a 100-point scale, a GPA in the low 80s or lower is a mediocre or low GPA.

Unfortunately, there are no "high school grades optional" colleges that we know about. Certainly, most colleges will claim to look at the whole picture—a complete profile—of a student during the admissions process; nonetheless, that whole picture always includes high school grades. While there can be reasons that high school grades are lower than the student is capable of earning—such as difficult family situations or personal problems or trauma—those reasons would have to be explained compellingly in an essay or an additional letter of some sort to the college. In short, it is really very difficult to explain away mediocre or low high school grades.

When a student has mediocre or low high school grades, it is ideal if that student happens to have high SAT or ACT scores. Then, the college can imagine that the student is bright, but perhaps had some reason for not performing as expected in high school classes. None of those reasons would be a great excuse, but some colleges will make an exception for such a student.

However, most students who have mediocre or low high school

grades do not have high SAT or ACT scores. For those students who have both mediocre or low high school grades and mediocre or low college admission test scores, the college choice with the highest cost-benefit ratio is probably a public two-year college—or maybe a public four-year college. By the way, great public four-year colleges can be just as difficult to get into as good private four-year colleges, so many of them are probably out of the running, too. If you look at the *average* high school GPAs of entering freshmen at many public state flagship universities, they are extraordinarily high—a 3.7 or 3.8 is not unheard of. Why again? Because many, many of the brightest students in a state want to attend—and do attend—the public state flagship university, for all the reasons we discussed earlier.

So, consider a public two-year community college, which gives a student a chance to erase a poor high school record with a better community college record. As we have said, a student who completes an associate's degree at a two-year college can transfer that entire degree—that is, all the credits that were earned in completing that degree—to a four-year college and be well on the way to earning a four-year bachelor's degree. When a student has earned that two-year associate's degree, the spotty high school record will become a thing of the past for most, if not all, four-year colleges.

To be sure, there are four-year public and private colleges that take students with mediocre or low high school grades. The question for parents is whether those colleges have as good a reputation as the kind of four-year public or private college a student might be admitted to after a successful experience at a two-year community college. It might also be a matter of money. Going for two years to a community college could save money that could then be put into a better four-year college for the final two years.

Of course, if you have still younger students at home, remind them now that there is no easy route to a great college if high school grades are poor.

Now that we have talked about *how selective* the colleges on your teenager's list should be, *how many* colleges should be on that list? Read on.

2. How Many Colleges?

Some students—though not many—know exactly where they want to go to college and believe they have a reasonable chance of being admitted to that one college. If you have such a teenager, here is what your teenager's college application process might look like.

If that one college, your teenager's perfect choice, has an **Early Decision** plan, he or she can apply to that college in the fall of the senior year (usually in early November). By doing that, however, he or she is agreeing to attend that college if accepted. An Early Decision offer of admission is binding on both the student and the college. Fortunately, however, if your teenager is *not* admitted when Early Decision offers are sent out (usually in December), there is still time to meet the application deadlines of most other colleges.

If your teenager's perfect college choice has an **Early Action** plan, he or she can also apply earlier and receive an answer earlier. Early Action works a bit like Early Decision, except that an offer of admission is *not* binding on the student. That is the crucial difference: A student can apply to more than one college with an Early Action plan, can also apply to other colleges with regular application deadlines, and does not have to accept an admissions offer as soon as it is given. Of course, if your teenager really wants to attend one college and that college has an Early Action plan and he or she is accepted, then the admission game is thankfully over.

Or your teenager's perfect college choice might have **rolling admissions**—meaning that applications are considered as they come in and decisions are made throughout the year. If the application is submitted early enough in the senior year and the decision is made fast enough by the college, then you *might* not have to consider other colleges. However, the exact schedule for reviewing applications at some colleges with rolling admissions is not knowable—meaning that a student might or might not get an acceptance quick enough to save the trouble of applying to other colleges.

For students whose perfect college choice does not have an Early Decision, Early Action, or rolling admissions plan, it would obviously be dangerous to apply just to one college on a regular deadline and not to look at some additional choices.

For all of those students who have not narrowed down their search to one college, how many applications should be made? Of course, there is no right answer to that question. Through some common sense thinking and discussion, we could probably agree that applying to just two or three colleges sounds like too few and that applying to, say, 15 colleges sounds like too many. The right answer for your teenager probably lies somewhere in between, depending on how much variety there is in the kinds of colleges you are considering and depending on how many deal breakers you and your teenager have.

For example, you can see right away that deciding to keep a

student close to home for college—maybe even within commuting distance—would limit the number of options available to that student (unless, of course, home is a major metropolitan area, like New York City). Such a student might feel that five or six applications would be a reasonable sample of the variety of opportunities available close to home. On the other hand, deciding to send a student away to college would open up an almost limitless number of options. Such a student might feel that even a dozen applications would not be an adequate sample of all the opportunities out there.

As you and your teenager add more deal breakers—that is, more restrictions on the colleges you want to consider—you probably will feel better that fewer applications can cover the remaining college options. For example, let's say your and your teenager have decided to limit your applications to small, private, four-year colleges in upstate New York that have French majors. With all of those restrictions, four or five applications might feel like plenty (though you might need a safety school, in that case, and perhaps a public one).

One more point: Your teenager should apply only to colleges that he or she actually knows something about and wants to attend. That might sound obvious to you, but it is not nearly so obvious to high school students as you might think. We find that students sometimes cannot explain why they are considering a certain college and sometimes cannot even find it on a map—even on a map of their home state. We have often used this minimum standard: If a student cannot find a college on a map, then he or she probably shouldn't apply to it. Such students need more help in applying their deal breakers to a list of possible colleges, in finding out about a good many of them, and then in narrowing down the possibilities to a reasonable number—probably about eight to 12.

3. To Visit or Not To Visit?

For many decades, one rite of passage for American high school-
ers and their parents alike has been the "college tour," where a parent takes an anxious or blasé teenager (depending on the teenager)
on a tour of colleges that might or might not turn out to be appealing schools to attend. During these college visits, there are campus
tours led by college students, often question-and-answer sessions
with administrators, sometimes a chance to sit in on a class or two,
and perhaps the nerve-wracking one-on-one admissions interview.

So, as you and your teenager enter the college applications process, let's ponder this question: How important are college visits?
You will actually hear, in our three options that follow, that the answer is always "very important." Only the *when* or *how* those visits
will occur is what we are going to talk about. College visits are . . .

- **Very important, so visit now . . .** because there is no substitute for standing in the main quadrangle or in a classroom building or in a dorm or on the soccer field or on the
  library steps. It is impossible to convey the feeling of a
  college's physical and social and intellectual environment
  without being there. Why would anyone want to sign up
  to spend two years or four years at a place that he or she
  had never seen? By the way, this is true for students who
  plan to live on campus and for students who plan to live
  off campus. Your teenager will spend a lot of time at the
  college—regardless of whether he or she is living in the
  dorms—and should want to get a feeling for its buildings
  and its grounds and its setting within its surroundings
  and, of course, its students, staff, and faculty.

Visiting colleges before applying to them makes a lot of

sense because even all colleges of a certain type are not the same. In other words, you cannot visit one or two private four-year colleges and, based on them, know what private four-year colleges are like. You cannot visit one or two public community colleges and, based on them, know what public community colleges are like. You cannot visit one or two urban campuses (or urban colleges with barely any "campus") and, based on them, know what urban colleges are like.

Visiting a college before applying might convince your teenager *not* to apply, thus saving you that time and effort and money. But, visiting colleges is not free—especially when they are not in your hometown. Many families cannot afford to take the time off or spend the travel money that it takes to make a college swing through several states—or even through your own state if it is too large to make an inexpensive day trip from one end to the other.

On the other hand, if you and your teenager have decided to limit your applications to colleges in your hometown or very close by, then you absolutely should visit before applying. Make sure you take a tour of the campus, that you talk with current students, and that you sit in on a class or two, if possible. There is no reason to miss out on this chance to find out what everyday life is like on that campus and how different it might feel from another college campus that could be just minutes away. For example, if you live in New York City and want to stay in New York City for college, you would find out how different the campuses of just these four-year colleges were if you were to visit them: New York University and The New School in Greenwich Village,

Columbia University and Barnard College in Morningside Heights, Fordham University at Lincoln Center, Hunter College in midtown, Pace University in downtown—and we have not left Manhattan yet. All of these schools are just a subway ride away for most New Yorkers.

- **Very important, but visit later ...** after acceptances have been received and your teenager is trying to decide which college to attend. After all, it is cheaper to pay the application fee for a college than to spend the money to visit it ahead of time (unless it is in your hometown).

If your teenager is accepted at more than one college, perhaps that is soon enough to spend the time and money to visit those colleges if you and your teenager are trying to decide among them. It might be that visiting your teenager's first choice is all that is needed—if the visit is successful and confirms that college to be the right one. That is a great cost-effective method.

- **Very important, but visiting is not an option...** because sometimes it is just not possible—financially or logistically—for a family to arrange for a campus visit to several colleges or even to one college, even after acceptances have come in.

In that case, you all can—and should—talk to anyone you can find who has visited any college still on your list as a kind of substitute for making the trip yourself. That might be a family friend, a high school friend, a teacher, a school administrator, a guidance counselor, or someone else. Some colleges have alumni/alumnae interviewers, who could serve this function nicely, too.

Firsthand impressions from someone who has walked on the campus in different seasons of the year, has seen inside the dorms, has talked with faculty or visited a class, has talked with current students or recent graduates, has eaten in the cafeteria, has attended a sports event or a cultural event—all of these impressions can help your teenager make a better decision about where to enroll. Ideally, at least some of those substitutes would be individuals who had been on the campus recently—and preferably someone with a more in-depth feel for the college than one can get from simply walking across the campus. A current professor or current student or recent graduate would be a great choice.

Remember, too, that it is not only about the physical surroundings, but also about the intellectual and social surroundings, which a casual visitor might not be able to pick up on so readily. Photographs in a brochure or on a website or even a virtual campus tour on a website might resolve your questions about the physical surroundings, but probably cannot answer your questions about the intellectual and social surroundings, which are more likely to affect your teenager's satisfaction with his or her college choice.

[8]

Making Your Teenager's List of Colleges

NOW LET'S REVIEW your deal breakers. Just transfer your checked boxes from Chapter 6 to those below so that you will have an easy-to-use set. As you make the transfer, think one last time about your deal breakers—because your next step is to apply them to colleges to see which colleges will make it onto your teenager's list.

1. Colleges Away from Home or Close to Home?
   - ❏ Only colleges away from home
   - ❏ Only colleges close to home
   - ❏ It doesn't matter—colleges away from home and/or close to home.
2. Two-Year or Four-Year Colleges?
   - ❏ Only two-year colleges
   - ❏ Only four-year colleges

❏ It doesn't matter—two-year and/or four-year colleges.

3. Public or Private Colleges?
   ❏ Only public colleges
   ❏ Only private colleges
   ❏ It doesn't matter—public and/or private colleges.

4. Large or Small Colleges?
   ❏ Only large colleges
   ❏ Only small colleges
   ❏ It doesn't matter—large and/or small colleges.

5. Urban, Suburban, or Rural Colleges?
   ❏ Only urban colleges
   ❏ Only suburban colleges
   ❏ Only rural colleges
   ❏ It doesn't matter—urban, suburban, and/or rural colleges.

6. Colleges with Certain Majors?
   ❏ Only colleges with certain majors
   ❏ It doesn't matter—colleges with or without certain majors.

7. Colleges with Certain Activities?
   ❏ Only colleges with certain activities
   ❏ It doesn't matter—colleges with or without certain activities.

8. Colleges with a Specific Mission?
   ❏ Only faith-based colleges
   ❏ Only single-sex colleges
   ❏ Only HBCUs
   ❏ It doesn't matter—faith-based colleges, single-sex colleges, and/or HBCUs.
   ❏ No faith-based colleges
   ❏ No single-sex colleges
   ❏ No HBCUs

9. Colleges with a Special Relationship to the Student's Family or High School?
   - ❏ Only colleges with a relationship to your family
   - ❏ Only colleges with a relationship to your teenager's high school
   - ❏ It doesn't matter—colleges with or without a special relationship to the family or high school.

Remember: If you'd like to download and print a summary version of the discussion guide, just sign up for our email list at http://policystudies.org/subscribe.

ABOUT THE AUTHORS

About Regina H. Paul. During more than 35 years at Policy Studies in Education, my nonprofit organization, I have worked hard to improve K–12 public education. I have developed K–12 curricula in all subjects, developed student examinations for school districts and states, evaluated new programs in over 400 school districts, and done market studies for over 150 colleges. I have consulted for state legislatures, state boards of education, state education departments, and foundations.

But some of my most interesting times and proudest achievements have come from projects I have done with parents. I have had the great pleasure of working with parents in big cities and medium-sized suburbs and tiny rural towns all across the U.S. Some did not graduate from high school, and some had advanced college degrees. Some had great jobs, and some had no jobs. But they all cared deeply about their children and what they were learning in school and what they would do when they graduated, and most of them were ready to pitch in.

Recently, I served as the chief consultant in the design and establishment of New York City's first public Early College high school with a career and technical education focus. Our school created an innovative trimester system that enabled students to complete high school in three years instead of four. Many of my best memories of my time at the school are of the parents, who stepped up and did whatever they could to make our school a success. As they got ready to send their children off to college (many a year early), we discovered they needed guidance. We gave it to them, one by one. Now, this book will do the same thing, but will allow us to reach many more parents much faster. We hope it helps.

About Marie G. Segares. I bring over 10 years of experience as an education manager and college professor to my role as co-host of the *NYCollegeChat* podcast. I've worked in academic affairs in both a public and a private college and in student affairs in a large university. This past year, I taught at two institutions of higher education—in New York and Texas—and I've taught online and face-to-face classes at several other institutions since 2008.

I've always been passionate about increasing access to college for a diverse group of students. Working with parents and students as a co-founder of a public Early College high school in New York City and as the director of its Early College program introduced me to many hard-working families who needed more information about the world of college and were overwhelmed by the many options. I talked with many parents about their hopes for their children and their concerns about college. I have enjoyed sharing my experiences—as an alumna of three institutions of higher education, as an education manager, and as a college instructor—with parents on the *NYCollegeChat* podcast every week.

About Policy Studies in Education. For over 40 years, Policy Studies in Education (PSE) has provided consulting services and technical assistance to schools, local and state boards of education, state education departments, state legislatures, federal education agencies, foundations, professional education associations, and public and private colleges.

We have conducted more than 500 data-based studies and program design projects in more than 40 states and abroad. These projects have spanned an array of topics, including curriculum and test development, program development and evaluation, parent advocacy, school governance, policy formulation and analysis, and administrative organization. In addition, we have trained tens of thousands of teachers and administrators and school board members across the U.S., often sponsored by state associations (such as the Texas Association of School Boards) or by national organizations (such as the American Association of School Administrators and National School Boards Association).

Currently, PSE is proud to sponsor *NYCollegeChat*, a free weekly podcast for parents, which is designed to help parents understand the world of college options available to their kids. Episodes are available at www.nycollegechat.org and on iTunes, Stitcher, and TuneIn.